The trustees of the
Pioneers Museum Foundation of Colorado Springs
are pleased to sponsor this second and limited edition
of Colorado Springs and Pikes Peak Country:
A Pictorial History.

This book is dedicated to the citizens
of our area, both past and present, whose
vision and pioneering spirit have contributed
so much to the dynamic qualities and rich fabric
of our beautiful community,
nestled in the shadow of Pikes Peak
and inspired by its grandeur.

William Council Holmes
Director
Colorado Springs Pioneers Museum

William D. Sinclair
President
Pioneers Museum Foundation

1

Design by Jamie Backus Raynor   Donning Company/Publishers • Norfolk/Virginia Beach

Colorado Springs
and Pikes Peak Country

By Rosemary Hetzler and John Hetzler

**Library of Congress Cataloging in
Publication Data:**

Main entry under title:

Colorado Springs and Pikes Peak Country:
a pictorial history.

Includes index.
1. Colorado Springs (Colo.)—
Description—Views.
2. Colorado Springs (Colo.)—History—
Pictorial works.
3. Colorado Springs region (Colo.)—
Description and travel—Views.
4. Colorado Springs region (Colo.)—
History—Pictorial works.
I. Hetzler, Rosemary.
F784.C7C68   978.8′56   81-5480
ISBN 0-89865-153-0   AACR2

Contents

Introduction

There have been books about Colorado Springs before, but never one like this. Here is a view of the historical development of Colorado Springs from prairie to oasis, from watering stop on the railroad to hub of an amazing number of Space Age industries, from a land of Indian superstitions to magical growth. The scope of this book is quite amazing. It captures that special appeal of the Pikes Peak region.

William Jackson Palmer, the city founder would hardly recognize his former home, but with the help of this book he could reconstruct its growth. Both the pioneers of Colorado Springs and her most recent arrivals will find something of interest here.

Colorado Springs has changed; in fact, it has changed more than once. The authors have captured many of those changes for us to see and understand. In addition they introduce us to many people who made the changes. The most amazing changes occur in the years between 1890 and 1920 when many people went from clerk to millionaire as a result of the Cripple Creek gold rush. The most recent rush to Colorado Springs did not bring the tremendous financial changes as before, but it certainly changed the town.

Fortunately, this book reminds us that no community is made up only of empty buildings or a big majestic peak. Most important are the people who all work together. The buildings are important, as is "our" mountain, but without our special people too, there would be less human appeal. This book illustrates that appeal, thoughtfully and skillfully captured in words and pictures.

Mel McFarland

Preface

Welcome to Colorado Springs. Come explore the history of this city from its marvelous photographic record. History is a fascinating word, the combination of *his* and *story*...history...

Welcome to the pictorial history of Colorado Springs!

Photographs prove history. They solidly support what words tell about them, and they fill the gaps that written language cannot cross. They are mirrors of history and reflect the finest nuances of the images they capture. Each one tells a remarkable story, and to understand these stories, you need only to listen with your eyes!

This land within the shadow of Pikes Peak—a new experience for thousands of newcomers—has been extensively photographed throughout its modern history. It has been written about narratively, as in James A. Michener's *Centennial,* and musically, as in Katharine Lee Bates' *America the Beautiful* which was inspired from the summit of Pikes Peak. The "fruited plain" is our city.

Collections of photographs have little value if they are not organized and made available. For many years the Pioneers' Museum, Tutt Library of Colorado College, Penrose Public Library, Stewart's Commercial Photographers, the Ute Pass Historical Society, and scores of historians have been assembling historic photographs to preserve and prove the remarkable past of Colorado Springs and the Pikes Peak region.

Here you will find the preserved pictorial history of the city as seen through the eyes of the people who photographed it. We attempt to present Colorado Springs as a dynamic city as experienced by people from all walks of life. Its strengths and its weaknesses shall be found in the remainder of these pages.

We dedicate this work to the land and the people who have built upon it; in every possible dimension and manner.

Rosemary I. Hetzler
and
John Inness Hetzler

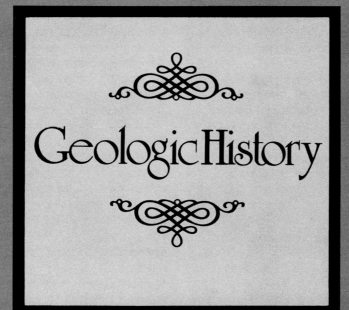

Geologic History

1 CHAPTER

The history of the Pikes Peak country begins with the rocks. A billion years of geologic history is available here, in one of the most complete and extensive records anywhere on earth. Museums worldwide display gems, minerals, and fossils collected within the shadow of Pikes Peak.

During this billion year time frame, the Pikes Peak region spent time as a sea bottom, a steaming dinosaur swamp, a Sequoia forest, and a scrubbing ground for glaciers during the Ice Ages. When the Rocky Mountains and Pikes Peak buckled and pushed upward during the Laramide Orogeny, some 63 million years ago, the incredibly thick sedimentary rocks were broken through and eroded away, exposing the complete record to the surface. The impressive tilting formed the Garden of the Gods and gave geologists the rare opportunity of studying a complete geologic record in one small geographic region. At the same time it created unforgettable scenery for both residents and tourists.

The geology has always been a magnet for drawing people to the Pikes Peak country. The Garden of the Gods was sacred territory to many Indian tribes who believed these rocks to be the home of supernatural spirits. In 1806 Lieutenant Zebulon Montgomery Pike sighted his namesake mountain from a point above the Arkansas River near Las Animas, Colorado. As the golden eagle flies, this is more than 100 miles away from the mountain. While he must have seen the Huatolla and summits of the Sangre de Christo range, it was Pikes Peak which caught his attention and drew him into the region. When General William Jackson Palmer came to the area in 1869, it was Pikes Peak and the springs of Manitou which inspired him to found Colorado Springs and make his home here. His interest in the regional geology prompted him to build a scaled-down replica of the sedimentary formations to the west of the city, called a geologic column. This model has been a matter of public interest since it was built, and can be seen in Monument Valley Park.

In 1891 on the western slope of Pikes Peak, Bob Womack discovered gold. The legends of the Cripple Creek goldfields are as numerous as the claims and as dynamic as the men who worked them. The significance of this factor on Colorado Springs is immeasurable.

Not only is the geologic record the first historical record of the region, but it is one of the most interesting. Its influence upon the geography of the Pikes Peak region and the growth of Colorado Springs cannot be ignored. It is an ongoing process, for as Colorado Springs grows, people constantly dig into new rocks. Imagine the excitement of the housewife who is digging in the garden and unearths a cephalopod. She gently brushes away the dirt and finds a lusterous mother-of-pearl coating; she wraps her fossil in a newspaper and rushes it down to the local museum as a major find. The joy of discovery is never old, and while this scene is practically a daily one in Pikes Peak country, it makes this special place even more special. It brings people the realization that natural history of immense magnitude has occurred here.

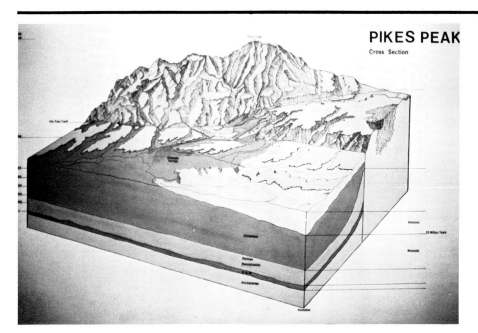

PIKES PEAK

Cross Section

A cross section of Pikes Peak and the geology beneath Colorado Springs shows the thick sedimentary deposits and the Pikes Peak batholith, spanning a billion years in formation. Artwork by Liliane Ross; courtesy of Pioneers' Museum

The geologic column in Monument Valley Park is a scaled-down reconstruction of the sedimentary formations to the west of and underneath Colorado Springs, using the actual stone from each represented formation. The column is one of many displays in Monument Valley Park, which was a gift to the city from General Palmer and was completed in November 1907. Photo from authors' collection

Sometime between the late Mississippian and mid-Pennsylvanian periods, 280 to 310 million years ago, a major **orogeny**, or mountain-building process, took place in this region. Two great mountain ranges, known as the Ancestral Rockies, were formed. The following erosion of the exposed Pikes Peak granite created the gigantic 4,000 foot thick Fountain Formation. In this 1915 picture, El Paso Boulevard near Manitou winds through the Fountain Formation. Photo courtesy of Pioneers' Museum

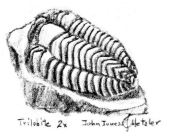

Trilobite 2x   John Iuves Hetzler

This trilobite was found in the limestone of the Manitou Formation in Williams Canyon, west of Colorado Springs. The Manitou Formation is a cavernous limestone formed some 450 million years ago during the Ordovician period, when this region was an oceanic bottom, similar to the Gulf of Mexico today. Artwork from authors' collection

Pikes Peak country was a sandy desert with a dry, windy climate 230 to 280 million years ago during the Permian period. The Ancestral Rockies had worn down considerably by this time. The Lyons Formation in the Garden of the Gods shows the cross bedding of the windblown sand dunes to the south of the Gateway Rocks. Photo courtesy of Pioneers' Museum

During the last part of the Jurassic period, 135 million years ago, the Pikes Peak country was a swampy lowland with sluggish streams flowing between plentiful freshwater lakes. Dinosaurs were common in this region during this period. Photo courtesy of Denver Museum of Natural History

A fossilized skeleton of Stegosaurus *was found in the Morrison Formation shales of Garden Park, on the south slope of the Pikes Peak massif. This specimen is on display at the Denver Museum of Natural History. Many other dinosaur skeletons were found here and they can be seen in museums across the United States. Photo courtesy of Denver Museum of Natural History*

This footprint left by Stegosaurus *is on display at the Denver Museum of Natural History. This was one of the most stupid creatures that ever lived, a ten-ton reptile that plodded through the Colorado swamps 140 million years ago. Photo courtesy of Denver Museum of Natural History*

Monument Creek is shown dropping over a shelf of Pierre shale. The Pierre Shale Formation underlies most of Colorado Springs and was deposited 130 million years ago when this region was the bottom of an inland sea. The Pierre shale contains numerous fossils, which are often found in newly developed areas. Photo from authors' collection

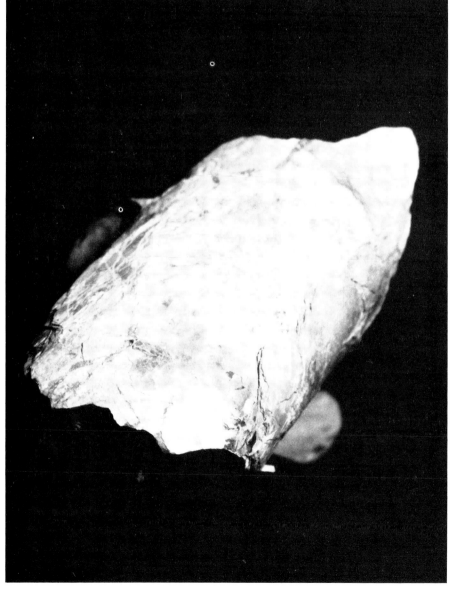

This cephalopod was found in the Pierre Shale Formation under Colorado Springs. This is one of the most commonly found fossils in the Pikes Peak region. Cephalopods were sea creatures which resembled squids and lived in a shallow sea which covered this region during the Cretaceous period, 130 million years ago. Photo from authors' collection

A hundred million years ago, Pikes Peak country was a steamy, primeval forest of cycads, tree ferns and dense vegetation. These forests were pressed under the Laramie Formation shales, with occasional lens-shaped layers of sandstone. The forests now are the extensive coal seams found in the lower part of the formation, north and east of Colorado Springs. Photo courtesy of Denver Museum of Natural History

Sometime during the Laramide Orogeny, a great block of Pikes Peak granite was thrust upward, through, and over the sedimentary formations to the east. Cheyenne Mountain, shown here, is the easternmost extension of this great block. Photo courtesy of Pioneers' Museum

Sixty million years ago as the Rockies were rising, the Pikes Peak region was a cool, moist, temperate rain forest, much like the modern redwood groves of northern coastal California today. On the western slope of Pikes Peak, an ancient volcano repeatedly erupted, burying Lake Florissant and creating one of the richest fossil beds on earth. Half of all known fossil butterflies are found here at Florissant Fossil Beds National Monument, as well as birds, fish, mollusks, insects, and plant life. These specimens from left to right are sequoia, beech, and redwood leaves, and cone, with foliage from living trees for comparison. Specimens and photo courtesy CCR

Clarence Coil did not make a fortune while panning for gold, but he did discover more museum-quality specimens of rare minerals from the Pikes Peak region than anyone else. Specimens of amazonite and goethite discovered by Coil are considered to be some of the finest ever found, and a barylite crystal dug by Coil is now property of the Smithsonian. Photo courtesy of Pioneers' Museum

The crater of Pikes Peak stands at 13,000 feet above sea level. There was no volcanism here though; rather this is a cirque carved by cookie-cutter-like glacial action during the Ice Ages. Photo courtesy of Pioneers' Museum

During the Quaternary period in the most recent million years, the climate changed and the Ice Ages began. Above 9,500 feet altitude on Pikes Peak, glaciers formed and carved out the U-shaped valleys on the west and the steep cliffs and cirques to the east, such as in the sunlit part of this picture. The shadow of Pikes Peak extends about fifty miles in this rare early morning photograph. Photo courtesy of Pioneers' Museum

Some of these trees began their lives before Jesus Christ was born. These are bristlecone pines (Pinus aristata-longaeva) growing at timberline on the Buffalo Peaks. The bristlecones are the oldest known living things—the oldest one in Nevada is 4,900 years old. Much historical knowledge can be gained from these trees. Dating methods were proven to be in error when compared with bristlecone wood, and, as a result, sites such as Stonehenge in England were proven to be much older than previously thought. On Hoosier Pass a grove of these and other conifers were cut down to build the town of Montezuma. While there are no records to prove exactly when this occurred, it is curious that the trees were cut off at heights of six feet or more above their bases, indicating there may have been a thick layer of snow on the ground, making it late winter or early spring when the forest was cut and the town built. Unfortunately, scenes like this photo are disappearing due to excessive cutting for firewood. Photo courtesy of Pioneers' Museum

In the fall of 1854 "Bad Indians" set fire to the forest, a method used to disturb the hunting for the Utes who were descending Ute Pass. Fierce winds blew the fire out of control, and it burned a seventy-mile long strip from Cheyenne Mountain to Wilkerson Pass. Early photographs show naked, barren, mountain slopes as in this 1873 painting of Colorado Springs by Walter Paris. Recovery has been slow and there are still visable signs from the Big Burn all across this section of the Front Range. Photo courtesy of Pioneers' Museum

Ute Pass sucked up the flames and smoke like a flue during the Big Burn of 1854. By the time the fire was burnt out, more than 1,000 square miles of timber had been destroyed. This 1880 photograph of Colorado Springs shows a stark, nearly treeless Front Range. Photo courtesy of Pioneers' Museum

The exact date of the Big Burn cannot be determined, but ring studies from damaged trees that survived, as well as accounts from Indians who were here at that time, indicate the year 1854. In this 1910 photo from the summit of Mount Manitou, fire-scarred trees can be seen along with the still-recovering bare slopes of Pikes Peak. Photo courtesy of Pioneers' Museum

One of the great white firs (Abies concolor) in North Cheyenne Canyon. The grove in White Fir Area is one of the finest stands of this tree in the world. Individual trees exceed 150 feet in height. The grove was spared from the great fire in 1854 when winds fanned the fire and caused it to jump from ridge to ridge, sparing the forests in the deepest canyon bottoms. Ring counts indicate that this grove is about 250 years old. Photo from authors' collection

Indians

The Apaches were split up into several bands: the Mescalero, San Carlos, Chiricahua, and Jicarilla. The latter tribe was friendly with the Utes which accounts for their occasional presence in the Pikes Peak region. Photo courtesy of Pioneers' Museum

2 CHAPTER

Indians who visited the Pikes Peak region long before the coming of the settlers were of two main types, the mountain tribes and the plains tribes. The Utes, known as the Mountain Indians, claimed this area as their own. Several tribes of Plains Indians came to this region in quest of good hunting. The most frequent of these were the Cheyennes and Arapahoes. Others were the Kiowas, Sioux, Comanches, Pawnees, and Jicarilla Apaches. The frequency and times of the year of their visits depended on the amount of hunting they could do. If buffalo, antelope, or deer were plentiful here, the Indians came and took advantage of the situation. No tribe made the Pikes Peak region its permanent home.

Sharp Nose, Arapahoe War Chief under Black Coal, became head chief after Black Coal's death. The Arapahoes and Cheyennes were of the same language group, the Algonquian, and were allied in more ways than other Plains Indians who visited the Pikes Peak region. The Pawnees were probably responsible for their present name, since they knew them as Tirapihu or Larapihu, which means traders. The Arapahoes were accustomed to barter and trade a great deal. Photo courtesy of Pioneers' Museum

APACHIE
SQAW
AND
PAPOOSE

29

The Cheyenne Indians were frequent visitors in the Pikes Peak region. They were reputed to be friendly, since they invited the French to trap for furs in their country. In 1860, however, warfare with the Sioux forced them to become nomadic and drift westward to become more dependent on buffalo for their livelihood. Photo courtesy of Pioneers' Museum

The Comanche Indians were among the earliest inhabitants of the Pikes Peak region but were eventually pushed south by enemy tribes. Their raids on the settlers brought them rich gains in horses and plunder. Photo courtesy of Pioneers' Museum

Chief Whiteman was a leader of the Kiowa tribe, which did not visit the Pikes Peak region frequently. The Sioux drove them from the plains into the mountains in 1803. There is little doubt that in this retreat they used Ute Pass. In 1806 the Kiowas occupied the country along the eastern base of the mountains, according to Lieutenant Zebulon Pike's journal. In 1867 they, along with the Cheyennes and Arapahoes, agreed to the Treaty of Medicine Bow and reluctantly went to their reservation in Oklahoma. Photo courtesy of Pioneers' Museum

The Pawnee Indians were an agricultural people who lived in the South. They raised corn, beans, squash, pumpkins, and other vegetables during the summer and went on hunting expeditions in the fall, which brought them to the Pikes Peak region. Photo courtesy of Pioneers' Museum

Sirvan was a Sioux of Red Cloud's tribe. The Sioux were frequently at war with the Utes which accounts for their being in the Pikes Peak region from time to time. During the intermittent periods of war and peace with the Cheyennes and Arapahoes, they often joined the latter in making war upon the Utes. Photo courtesy of Pioneers' Museum

Ko-Mus belonged to the Uintah band of Utes. His ancestors roamed largely over the central and western sections of Colorado using Ute Pass Trail to bring them into the Pikes Peak region and the plains area. After the Spaniards introduced horses to the region, they hunted on horseback and proved themselves equals of the Plains Indians both in hunting and in warfare. Photo courtesy of Pioneers' Museum

After the Meeker Massacre the Utes were confined to reservations. Treaties in 1868, 1874, and 1880 between the Utes and the United States Government forced them to cede all lands claimed by them. They went to a reservation in southwestern Colorado. Pictured are: Ignacio, Honorable Carl Schurz, Vortez, Ouray, General Adams, and Chipita, wife of Ouray. Photo from authors' collection

Photograph of oil painting by Charles Craig commissioned in 1903 to be painted for the El Paso County Courthouse. It now hangs in the Pioneers' Museum

Age of
Possession
& Exploration

Both France and Spain claimed the Pikes Peak region until 1763. Sieur de La Salle, carrying the flag of France down the Mississippi River on 9 April 1682, laid claim to all land drained by the great river. Thus the king of France acquired a new empire named Louisiana. The Spanish too, established a claim in the name of Phillip V. In 1706 Juan de Ulibarri went from Santa Fe, New Mexico to El Caurtelejo in eastern Colorado to capture run-away Indian slaves. The royal ensign, Don Francisco de Valdez, a member of the party, declared that the great settlement of Santo Domingo of El Cuartelejo belonged to the Spanish monarch. There were no serious challenges to Spain's control of Colorado until late in the seventeenth century when the French, in search of furs, began pushing farther westward from their outposts on the Mississippi River.

At the close of the French and Indian War in 1763, rivalry between France and Spain for the land which included Colorado came to an end. France added her territorial claims west of the Mississippi to those of Spain. All of Colorado then became undisputed Spanish land. In 1800 Spain re-ceded the Louisiana territory to France. Napoleon I sold it to the United States three years later when agents of President Jefferson made the famous Louisiana Purchase, for $15,000.

In 1819 the United States and Spain agreed that the boundary between Mexico and Louisiana should be the Arkansas River to its source and then westward to the crest of the Continental Divide. Thus the Pikes Peak region once belonged to the king of France, the king of Spain, Napoleon I, and finally to the United States.

Lieutenant Zebulon Montgomery Pike was the first United States explorer to come into the Pikes Peak region who kept accurate accounts of his journey and was the first to describe the peak which bears his name. Acting under orders from General James Wilkerson, Lieutenant Pike set out from Belle Fontaine north of St. Louis on 11 July 1806. The purpose was to restore to their own people a band of Osage Indians who had been held captive by the Potawatomi of Illinois and to take home Osage and Pawnee chiefs who had been to Washington, D.C. to visit the president of the United States.

Major Stephen H. Long, under orders from John C. Calhoun, Secretary of War, set out from the present site of Omaha, Nebraska, during the summer of 1820. He was to explore to the source of the Platte River and then, by way of the Arkansas and Red rivers, move down to the Mississippi. Dr. Edwin James, who accompanied Major Long, wrote of the Pikes Peak region: "In regard to this extensive section of the country, I do not hesitate in giving the opinion that it is almost wholly unfit for cultivation and of course uninhabitable by a people dependent on agriculture. This region viewed as a frontier may prove of infinite importance to the United States serving as a barrier to prevent extension of our population westward."

General John C. Fremont was the last of the famous explorers to visit the Pikes Peak region during his expedition in 1843. Fremont made several explorations into the West over a period of eleven years. Some excursions he made as an official of the United States government and others he made on his own initiative. His main objective was to find a more favorable route to the Pacific for building a railroad than the Oregon or Santa Fe trails. On each of his five expeditions he touched Colorado territory.

Lieutenant Zebulon Montgomery Pike was one of the first European-Americans to see Pikes Peak. Lieutenant Pike was assigned to explore the headwaters of the Arkansas River in behalf of the United States under the administration of President Thomas Jefferson, beginning in July 1806. Photo from authors' collection

General John C. Fremont and his party followed Bijou Creek into what is known as Bijou Basin, located about six miles north of Peyton, Colorado. Many old-timers in the vicinity maintain that the rock known as Fremont's Fort in the basin was the site of Fremont's camp. Photo courtesy of Pioneers' Museum

This is an early view looking east from the summit of Pikes Peak, elevation 14,110 feet. The picture was probably taken in November, around 1890. At this time of year, arctic weather scours the rocky summit. A sea of clouds covers the Colorado Springs basin a mile-and-one-half below; a frequent event during the early winter here. In November 1806 Lieutenant Zebulon Montgomery Pike recorded such a sea-cloud in his journal during the unsuccessful attempt to climb the mountain. Photo from authors' collection

Trappers

4 CHAPTER

Although the French trappers exploited the streams in the Pikes Peak region for fur-bearing animals to some extent, this region was not used as much as the regions farther north. The source waters of the Missouri and the Green rivers were more accessible and provided a means of transporting their catch. The streams in the Pikes Peak region carried more water than they do today, since no water was stored for the population of the larger cities or for irrigation projects.

Perhaps the typical trapper was uncouth in a manner of speaking, but he was wise in other ways. Well trained to read the signs of the wilderness, the signs of the bear and the beaver, the footprints of the Indian, and the seldom traversed trails, he would live for long periods of time in the wilderness with no help from the outside. He had the woodsman's sense of direction and was able to live on the resources of the country. He knew how to deal with the friendly Indians and how to hide from the hostile ones.

The trappers were the real pathfinders of the region, and they made it easier for the explorers and settlers who came later. Many of them served as guides for explorers such as Pike, Long, and Fremont. They knew the easiest passes through the mountains, the best fording places along the rivers, and the most desirable watering places on the plains.

The fur trade began to decline about 1850. As fashionable French silk hats and seal-skin coats began to be more popular than the "beaver," the demand lessened for these pelts. Then, of more importance, was the scarcity of animals to trap and kill. The hunters killed off great numbers of buffalo, many times just for sport. The herd began to decrease at an alarming rate, causing serious hardships for the Indians who depended on the buffalo for food. By the time the "1859-ers" came into the Colorado territory looking for gold, the trading posts were in ruins. Thus, a romantic era of history came to an end.

Jim Baker was in the employ of the American Fur Company for a time and was an independent trapper as well. He operated a toll road at the Clear Creek Crossing near Denver in the early days. He also acted as a guide for General Fremont and was one of the best-known trappers in Colorado. Photo courtesy of Pioneers' Museum

James Beckworth was another trapper in the early days of Colorado territory. For a long time he lived among the Crow Indians and led them in wars against the Cheyenne and Sioux. Later he took up land in the territory, but when he thought too many people were coming into the West, he went back to live with the Indians. Photo courtesy of Pioneers' Museum

Christopher (Kit) Carson was the most celebrated character among the trappers. His career included working as an independent trapper, a hunter, a guide for General Fremont, and serving as a colonel of the New Mexico Volunteers during the Civil War. He was also chief of scouts for General Kearney, a rancher, an Indian agent, and even a sheep driver. During the gold rush in California he drove more than 6,000 sheep here from New Mexico where he realized a profit of five dollars per head. Fort Carson in Colorado Springs is named for this famous scout. Photo courtesy of Pioneers' Museum

It took $5,000 worth of beaver pelts to keep Walter Devereux warm in 1888. He and his Broadmoor family were active in developing the mining industry in Colorado. Photo courtesy of Pioneers' Museum

Henry Harkens, murdered by the Espinoza Gang on 19 March 1863, built his cabin south of Colorado Springs off of what is now Highway 115. His burial plot was later enclosed by a white picket fence. Photo from authors' collection

Tom Tobin killed the notorious Espinoza bandits during the early territorial days of Colorado. These bandits held up stages, killed passengers, and shot down persons at lonely ranch houses, spreading terror over a large part of the West. He single-handedly trailed them and brought them to justice in true western-style in 1863. He was a lifelong friend of Kit Carson.

He was given this handmade beaded suit by Chipita, wife of Ute Chief Ouray. Photo courtesy of Pioneers' Museum

Uncle Dick Wootton's search for beaver carried him into unexplored parts of the Rocky Mountains. He is thought to have been the first cattle rancher in the Arkansas Valley. A toll road over Raton Pass from Colorado into New Mexico was operated by him. At one time he owned the Manitou Soda Springs. Photo from authors' collection

James Jefferson, Southern Ute tribal historian, is shown in front of the smallest museum in the world. The Ute Pass Trail Museum, operated by the Ute Pass Historical Society, covers the history of the trail for which El Paso County was named and over which passed the Ute Indians, trappers, traders, explorers, and the gold seekers that made Colorado famous. Photo courtesy of Ute Pass Historical Society

Colorado City

5 CHAPTER
1859~1917

Colorado City, the first permanent settlement in the Pikes Peak region, came as a direct discovery of gold in Colorado. The name given the town at first was El Dorado (a Spanish term meaning gold region).

During the period 1859-1861, the Pikes Peak country meant anyplace within sight of Pikes Peak—a radius of about 100 miles. The Pikes Peak region became the objective of thousands who sought to "strike it rich." Some did find gold, settled down, sent for their families, and became influential citizens. The hordes of others who came because of the exaggerated reports that the barren slopes were full of gold and silver were disappointed and returned home.

With the discovery of gold in South Park, a company was formed and a claim established covering the site of the short-lived El Dorado. Some 1,280 acres were included within the jurisdiction of the El Paso Claim Club by December 1859. The community was named Colorado City and it remained as such until 1917 when its residents voted to be annexed to Colorado Springs.

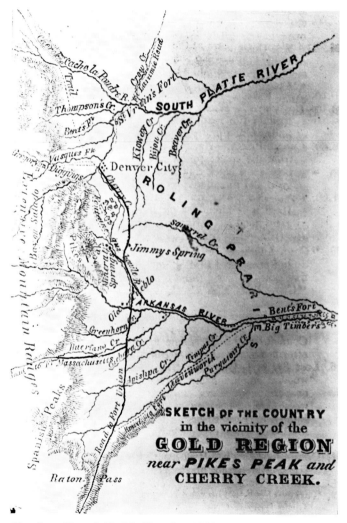

Map from Marcy's Prairie Traveler, *1859.*
Photo from authors' collection

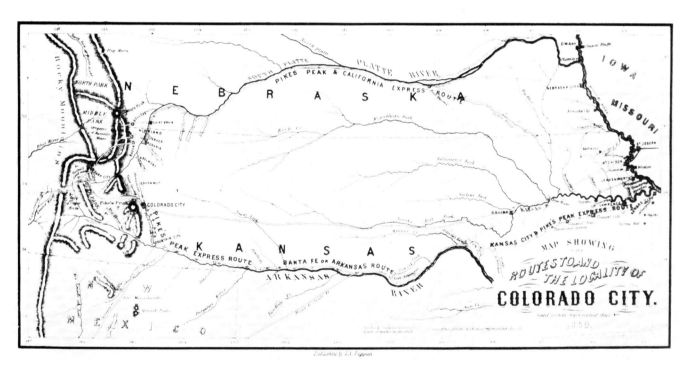

The organization of a group known as the Lawrence Party had a direct influence in starting a settlement in the immediate Pikes Peak region. This party was organized and left Leavenworth, Kansas, on 19 May 1858. There were about fifty persons in the party, including two women. They moved up the Arkansas and headed for Pikes Peak, prospecting the streams in the immediate vicinity of Colorado Springs. They spent several days here, their headquarters being on Camp Creek near the Garden of the Gods. The origin of the name Camp Creek is thereby accounted for; the party of prospectors set up their camp along the creek that bears this name. Photo from authors' collection

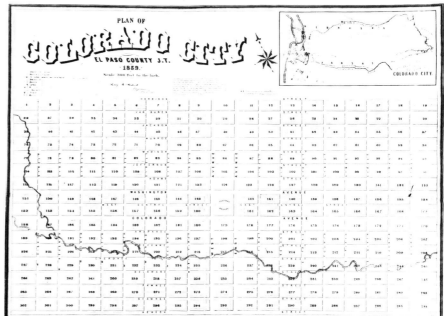

Shown is the plan of Colorado City, El Paso County, and Jefferson Territory in 1859. Streets have been renamed and renumbered since this map was made. Photo from authors' collection

Pikes Peak or Bust. A dream of gold and a pioneering spirit brought the covered wagon people to Colorado City in 1859. This painting by Charles Craig hangs in the Pioneers' Museum. Photo courtesy of Pioneers' Museum

In 1860 Fannie McConnell lived in this house, built by A. Z. Sheldon, at 1928 Washington Street, Colorado City. Drawing by Harry Dugger; from an early photograph

According to an article in the Colorado Springs Gazette, *21 October 1905, Mrs. Fannie McConnell was a noted rebel spy under General Bragg. Her maiden name was Fannie Wright and she was known to many leaders of the rebel army as one of the most trusted secret agents of the Confederacy. At the close of the Civil War she married J. McConnell, a prosperous farmer. They settled in Texas and later moved to Colorado City. Drawing by Harry Dugger; from an early photograph*

A wagon train is shown descending Ute Pass. The following is an excerpt from a letter written at Colorado City, 1861: "Since my arrival here the rush to the mines has been steadily increasing. On account of the only pass through the mountains yet discovered being through this town, it promises to be an important point, especially should the report from the mines be substantial. From one hundred to one hundred twenty wagons pass through town daily." Photo courtesy of Pioneers' Museum

The Colorado City and Denver Express Line was established by H. G. Weiling in 1861. He advertised that his coaches ran every week, carrying the United States mail, express matters, and passengers. Photo from authors' collection

The family of Robert A. Finley is shown at their home in Colorado City. Finley was elected clerk and recorder of Colorado City in November 1861 on a white ballot of 150 votes. Photo from authors' collection

The William F. Dixon Ranch lay partly on the western end of Broadmoor extending into Stratton Park and up the eastern slope of Cheyenne Mountain. The land was claimed by Dixon in 1862. Mrs. Dixon is shown in their two-room cabin. After his death in 1907, a part of the property was sold and eventually became El Pomar, home of Mr. and Mrs. Spencer Penrose. Photo from authors' collection

This lithograph of Colorado City in 1866 shows Pikes Peak in the background. Photo from authors' collection

This small log building was erroneously referred to as the State Capitol building. In reality it was the first drug store and also served as the office of Dr. James P. Garvin, the first physician of Colorado City. In 1869 it was used by Irving Howbert, county clerk; then it became a Chinese laundry. The building was owned by M. S. Beach, one of the founders of Colorado City. Now restored, it is located in Bancroft Park on West Colorado Avenue and bears the following identification: Erected 1859, Pioneer County Office. Photo from authors' collection

This photo of Colorado City in 1870 with Pikes Peak in the background shows the El Paso House (center). It was also known as the Holmes House and as the Baird and Smith Hotel. The building across the street belonged to Tappan and Company and is credited with being the first frame building. Photo from authors' collection

Members of the El Paso County Pioneer's Association, in costume, pose at the dedication of the Old Colorado City Fort and Stockade. The marker was erected by the Colorado State Historical Society from the Mrs. J. N. Hall Foundation, the El Paso County Pioneer's Association, and the city of Colorado Springs. The fort had been built by pioneers of Colorado City for defense against Indians in 1864 and 1868. Photo courtesy of Pioneers' Museum

Authors' sketch of the Old Colorado City Fort and Stockade, based on descriptive information. Contrary to the Hollywood version of western pioneer forts, the logs were not stacked horizontally, but placed vertically. A stacked fort would have to have been built from logs of equal size, and the scarcity of trees in this region made such selection an impractical option. Vertical placement allowed logs of unequal size to be used, and so construction was more quickly and easily accomplished. Drawing from authors' collection

The Glass Works was built just south of Colorado City in 1889, on twenty acres in the area of present-day Wheeler Street. Jerome Wheeler, Adolph Busch, Louis Ehrich, Jefferson A. Hayes, and General Charles Adams financed it. An immediate market was the Manitou Mineral Water Bottling Company. Photo from authors' collection

57

To produce the bottles at the Glass Works, Bohemian glass blowers were brought to Colorado City. Each produced sixty dozen handblown bottles a day. After the factory was destroyed by fire in 1892, plans were begun to rebuild on a smaller scale. In 1893 silver was demonetized, crippling the resources of the owners and stockholders. When the business ended in 1898, the glass blowers left to seek employment in the glass factories in Pittsburg. Photo courtesy of Pioneers' Museum

The Standard Mill was the second mill built in Colorado City after the discovery of gold in Cripple Creek in 1891. The first mill constructed was the Philadelphia, the third was the Golden Cycle, and the fourth was the Portland.

The first process for the extraction of gold and other minerals from Cripple Creek ore was the chlorination method. Later the cyanide method was adopted. Drawing hangs in Pioneers' Museum; photo from authors' collection

The cyanide process of extracting gold from the ore was a success from the start at this mill. Other mills in the area could not compete in this process and ceased operation.

In 1949 the Golden Cycle agreed to donate one-third of the amount of gold necessary to resurface the State Capitol dome, a job that would cost $21,000. Today it would cost $375,000.

The mill ceased operation around 1949 and all that remains today is the smokestack. Photo from authors' collection

STANDARD AND COLORADO PLANTS, COLORADO CITY COLO.
UNITED STATES REDUCTION AND REFINING COMPANY.

copyright 1901 by William ...

59

This photo shows Reidel's Tailor Shop in Colorado City, about 1900. Many ball gowns for milady in fashionable Colorado Springs came from this shop. Note the spiral cloak hangers by the chandelier and the muddy shoes under the stove. Photo courtesy of Pioneers' Museum

This aerial view shows West Colorado Springs about 1920, before the Pleasant Valley addition was built and the Mesa was developed.

The White House Ranch, now part of the Colorado Springs Park Department, is seen as two white dots at the end of 31st Street and Camp Creek, at right of the Garden of the Gods rocks. Photo from authors' collection

Photo shows South 29th Street in West Colorado Springs, about 1925. The Midland School is the white building off the street at right. It was abandoned and sold in 1980 and became a private school. Photo from authors' collection

Irving Howbert arrived at Pikes Peak in 1860 at the age of fourteen, with his father, William Howbert, a Methodist minister. He served as El Paso County Clerk in 1869 and became president of the First National Bank in 1880.

In 1925 the citizens of Colorado Springs and the state of Colorado gave a dinner for Howbert in recognition of the publishing of his Memories Of A Lifetime in the Pikes Peak Region. *Photo courtesy of Pioneers' Museum*

New streetcar tracks are laid along West Colorado Avenue in the early 1920s. Looking toward the east. Photo courtesy of Pioneers' Museum

Founding
and Early
Development

6 CHAPTER 1871~1890

Colorado Springs was the dream of William Jackson Palmer, Civil War hero and promoter of the Denver and Rio Grande Western Railroad.

As soon as General Palmer was assured that the Rio Grande line would be built to Colorado City, he began planning the city which became Colorado Springs. The Mountain Base Investment Fund was organized to raise money for the railroad in 1870. This was the parent company of the Colorado Springs Company organized six months later to raise capital to construct irrigation ditches, lay out streets, plant trees, and aid the building of a hotel in the new town. The company planned to sell the tracts and lots to new arrivals on small payments distributed over several years. About one-half of the capital of this company was raised in America among Palmer's friends in Philadelphia, and the remainder was raised in Europe, chiefly among the associates of Palmer's friend, Doctor W. A. Bell.

The first stake was set in place 31 July 1871 at the southeast corner of Pikes Peak and Cascade avenues. The city plot contained seventy blocks, each 400 feet square.

Under the guiding hand of General Palmer an attractive city with broad avenues and ample streets developed. Trees were planted, and canals and a network of ditches were constructed to irrigate them. Palmer chose the site of Monument Valley Park and laid plans which gave the modern city magnificent system of parks, drives, and mountain trails.

Lured by gold, Governor Alexander Cameron Hunt crossed the plains nine times by wagon or stagecoach when the journey took three months. Hunt served the territory in Congress and then became the fifth governor.

General Palmer said Hunt blazed the trails for the Denver and Rio Grande Railroad engineers with his knowledge of the territory. Photo from authors' collection

William Jackson Palmer traveled widely
and made such an impression in European
circles by his culture, force of character,
and high aspiration, that he influenced a
considerable number of men and women of
high educational and moral thought to come
to the Rocky Mountain region from the
older civilizations of Europe, during the
early settlement of Colorado Springs.

In reviewing the tributes made to
William Jackson Palmer by people who
knew him well, the points of his character
which stand out above all others are his
extreme modesty, his good judgement, and
the foresight which seemed almost to stamp
him as a being of a superior kind.

The words chosen so carefully for the
memorial tablets which honor this great
American citizen should be especially
familiar to those of us who live in, and who
visit, the city that was so dear to him and
for which he did so much.
1836 William Jackson Palmer 1909
"Union County general, pioneer
railroad builder, prophet of
Colorado's greatness. He mapped the
routes of three transcontinental
railways, supervised the building of
the first road to Denver, organized
and constructed the Denver and Rio
Grande Railroad, stimulated the
state's industries, cherished its
beauties, founded Colorado Springs,
fostered Colorado College, and served
our sister Republic of Mexico with
sympathy and wisdom in developing
its national railways." Photo from
author's collection

At the driving of the stake for the new town 31 July 1871 at 8:00 a.m., a small company of people stood about. They called for a speech from General Robert A. Cameron, who stood on a pile of nearby lumber and eloquently spoke of the health-giving elements of the climate, the natural advantages, and the magnificent scenery. General Cameron's belief in the future of the town was as firm as General Palmer's. He said, "In a few years as we look out from the porch of some magnificent temple, see the wealth and beauty spread at our feet, we shall be glad that we can look back to this day, and to this simple yet suggestive ceremony and say, 'All this I saw, and part of this I was.'" Photo from Rhoda Wilcox Collection

E. S. Nettleton was engineer of the Colorado Springs townsite in 1871. He engineered the Fountain and Monument irrigation canals, and under his direction the dam for the Fountain ditch was placed about one-half mile above Colorado City. The ditch was carried eleven-and-a-half miles through Colorado City and to the northern part of Colorado Springs. Water wells were dug for drinking, and water was also obtained from the springs in Monument Valley. Water was hauled and sold from barrels. Photo from Rhoda Wilcox Collection

W. E. Pabor served as secretary of the Fountain Colony, started in 1871. After he built his home at the corner of Cascade and Bijou streets, Mrs. William J. Palmer rented it for a school to serve the colonists' children. The school formally opened on 13 November 1871 and was conducted by Mrs. Liller, the first full-time school teacher.

For a while, Mr. Pabor edited the Gazette newspaper and wrote many articles as well as poetry. Photo from Rhoda Wilcox Collection

The Manitou Springs were originally named La Font *by General William Jackson Palmer who plotted Manitou in 1871. The name was changed to Manitou when William Blackmore and General Cameron visited them and drew inspiration from some Ute Indians who were there. Actually the legends and stories concerning the Indians, Manitou, and the springs are mostly just that—stories without one iota of truth—but they do make nice stories. Photo courtesy of Pioneers' Museum*

After the Denver and Rio Grande Railroad was organized, a meeting was held and the Colorado Springs townsite company was organized. The group arrived at the site of Colorado Springs a few days later ready to begin the survey. General Robert Cameron was engaged to manage the town company. Forty or fifty persons, who proposed casting their fortunes with the new town, arrived and took up residence in tents and temporary frame structures. Photo courtesy of Pioneers' Museum

This is the Montezuma, first engine of the narrow gauge Denver and Rio Grande Railroad. Regular service between Denver and Colorado Springs began 1 January 1872. Photo from authors' collection

During the years just after Palmer founded Colorado Springs, the Royal Gorge War raged between the Denver and Rio Grande and Santa Fe railroads. The culmination took place in court, but the deadline during the fight (shown here), while posed, did show that both railroads meant business. Forts were built at each end of the gorge, and gunfighters were hired to protect railroad interests. The Denver and Rio Grande won the court battle and right of way, and in 1883 its president, General Palmer, retired. Photo courtesy of Denver Public Library, Western Collection

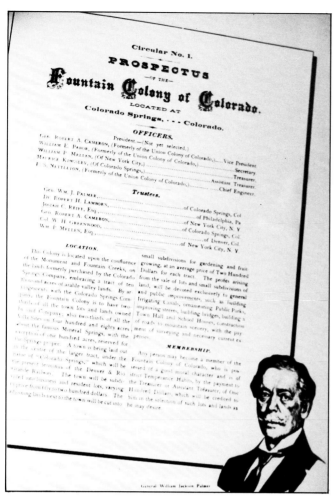

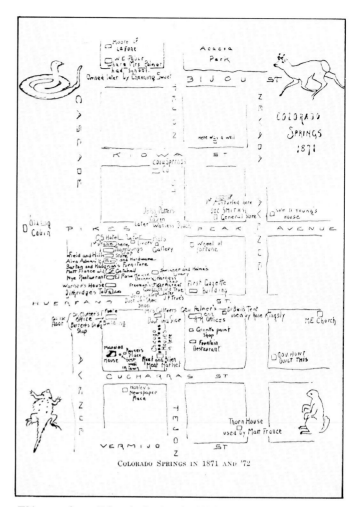

This circular was issued by the Fountain Colony, forerunner of the Colorado Springs Company, to advertise the new enterprise. It should be noted that two townsites were laid out, at Manitou, surrounding the mineral springs, and at Colorado Springs. Photo from authors' collection

This map shows Colorado Springs in 1871 and marks the sites of the first buildings. Photo from authors' collection

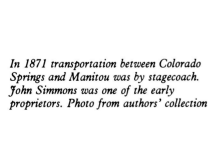

In 1871 transportation between Colorado Springs and Manitou was by stagecoach. John Simmons was one of the early proprietors. Photo from authors' collection

An 1872 picture shows Pikes Peak Avenue. When the survey crew was laying out the town, General Cameron said, "Point your transit toward Pikes Peak then turn it around and you will have Pikes Peak Avenue."

The Colorado Springs Hotel is at the far end of the street. The building in the foreground is a photography shop.

To irrigate the newly-planted trees, the El Paso Canal was built. On 13 January 1872, the ditch water ran completely through the town, and people planted trees, gardens, and lawns. Photo from authors' collection

Matt France served on the first governing board of Colorado Springs. When a formal order incorporating the town of Colorado Springs was made on 2 September 1872, it remained a town governed by the board until 1876. The five men who composed the board the first year were the following: William B. Young, president; R. A. Cameron; Edward Copley; John Potter; and Matt France. In 1875 the population was more than 3,000, large enough to make Colorado Springs a city. Photo from authors' collection

73

This photo shows the Widefield School in District #3. The grout building was built prior to 1871 by patrons of the district, among whom were Adam Paster and Richard Gains. A corner fell out during a session of school in 1887, and the new building was erected near the same site. In the picture are: Buelah De Graff, Tracy De Graff, Joseph Cell, Mattie Cell, Gertrude Cell, Amanda Cell, Herbert Betts, and Mrs. Kittie Paster Fryhofer, teacher. Photo courtesy of Pioneers' Museum

Governor A. C. Hunt and Major John H. McDowell, of the Denver and Rio Grande Railroad, built a log cabin to use as headquarters at the new townsite. The building then became the Log Cabin, an eating house. It was patronized by many prominent early settlers.

This 1871 photograph shows: Governor A. C. Hunt, Mrs. Elizabeth Hunt McDowell, E. J. Eaton, Mrs. Helen McDonald Malburn, Major John H. McDowell and John C. McDowell, sitting with rifle. Photo courtesy of Pioneers' Museum

This is the dinner menu of the Log Cabin, 25 December 1871. Photo courtesy of Pioneers' Museum

The Colorado Springs Hotel opened 1 January 1872. An early register shows the arrival of 3,647 persons, a result of the advertising the region received. Inhabitants from almost every state in the union came as well as fifty-four from England, two from France, one from Australia, and one from the Republic of Mexico. Rose and Maurice Kingsley, daughter and son of Canon Charles Kingsley of Westminster Abbey are at left front in the picture. Rose was important in organizing the cultural affairs of the new town, and Maurice was assistant treasurer of the Fountain Colony.

After the Antlers Hotel was built, the Colorado Springs Hotel became the Antlers Annex in 1884. Later it was sold and removed to 617 South Nevada Avenue where it became an apartment building. It was remodeled and is now occupied by Pikes Peak Legal Services. Photo from authors' collection

John Potter, one of the first arrivals in the new town and one of the first to build a cabin, became its first postmaster in 1872. The population was less than 1,000 at that time, but when the mail was distributed the entire population seemed to turn out for the event. Everybody had letters from the East or wanted to send letters to their Eastern connections. John Potter's yearly salary was $400. Photo courtesy of Pioneers' Museum

Eliphalet Price came to Colorado Springs in late 1872, for his health. He was a lawyer by profession but loved the newspaper business and frequently submitted stories, the best known being the Pikes Peak Rat Story. *It was one of the most remarkable hoaxes that ever succeeded in attaining world notoriety. Judge Price and the hero of the story, Sergeant John T. O'Keefe, were quite well-known local characters. Price's* Satan's Visit to Colorado Springs, *written in 1873, provided the townsfolk with subtle humor. Photo from authors' collection*

Dr. William Bell came to St. Louis from London to investigate some new medical findings. He heard about the Kansas Pacific Railroad survey and signed up as a photographer, this being the only position open. General William J. Palmer was the engineer in charge of construction of the Kansas Pacific, and through this association Palmer and Bell became lifelong friends and business associates. They devised a plan for buying land along the proposed railroad route and later selling it to provide money for building the railroad and to take care of the needs of the citizens in the settlements which became Colorado Springs and Manitou.

This is a picture of Dr. and Mrs. William Bell about 1875. Photo courtesy of Pioneers' Museum

The United States Army Signal Station on the summit of Pikes Peak. This was the first such station, built in 1873. The large rocks on the roof were put there to hold the roof down during high wind, but the effort was in vain. The relentlessly harsh weather ruined this and other buildings on the summit, destroying them more quickly than they could be maintained. Photo courtesy of Pioneers' Museum

The first meeting of the volunteer firemen was held in January 1873. At their second meeting a month later the company changed its name to the Colorado Springs Fire Company since the original name, Hook and Ladder Company, did not apply because they did not have a ladder truck. On 29 January 1894 the city council met in secret session and passed a lengthy ordinance disbanding the volunteer company and creating a department of paid firemen.

The bell of the volunteer department is the base for the flagpole at the central fire station and bears a plaque commemorating the volunteers. Photo from authors' collection

The grasshopper scourge of 1874 was the worst such invasion Colorado Springs has ever seen. Modern gardeners should feel fortunate that they do not have a plague such as this to contend with. Photo courtesy of Pioneers' Museum

A source of lumber in early days was the Jerome A. Weir sawmill in the Pinery, known as Black Forest. This painting by J. R. Duncan hangs in the Pioneers' Museum. Photo courtesy of Pioneers' Museum

Jerome Weir is shown hauling lumber from his sawmill in the Pinery. He started this business in the late 1860s and supplied lumber for some of the first houses in Colorado Springs, Colorado City, and Manitou. The mill closed down in 1882. Photo courtesy of Pioneers' Museum

In the horse-drawn vehicle days, long wagons had to be taken apart, as shown in this picture, in order to cross a deep gully. Photo from authors' collection

On the northeast corner of Tejon and Huerfano streets (Colorado Avenue), the first two-story building was erected. The lower floor served as the newspaper office, and the upper floor was used as a public hall. The famous George Rignold and his company put Colorado Springs on the Shakespearean map of the world when they presented King Henry IV *there on 23 May 1878. Photo from authors' collection*

The Seven Lakes Hotel, in the tarn-dotted valley between Pikes Peak and Almagre Mountain, was built on the Seven Steps Road by Quincy King and Mr. Welch in 1879. Author Helen Hunt Jackson stayed here often and described the manager of the hotel as, "a strange man of Mohammedan, sacred dervish tendencies who practices semi-medical, semi-religious medicine by the laying on of hands and administering the milk cure." Photo courtesy of Pioneers' Museum

The Seven Lakes Valley and Pikes Peak as seen from 12,367 foot Almagre Mountain, about 1925. Photo from authors' collection

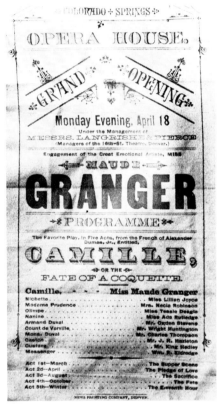

James Head, an English marksman, took part in a shooting match in Colorado Springs between England and America in 1879. England won 31-29. Photo from authors' collection

This program for the stage play Camille, was printed with yellow lettering on white satin. Photo from authors' collection

Camille, starring Maude Granger, was the first performance in the Colorado Springs Opera House in 1881. It was the stage version of La Traviata, a poor choice since while Camille was coughing away her last moments on the stage, half of the audience was coughing from consumption, the disease that brought many people to Colorado Springs seeking "the cure." Photo from authors' collection

Phil Struble's Barber Shop was located at 12 South Tejon Street in 1900. Frank H. Chaney, father of Lon and John Chaney, was a barber at this shop. Others in the photo are: James Howard, Ike Gary, John Newman, Jeff Wyatt, Sam Dunlap, Ike Phillips, Ray Hotchkiss, Sherman Smith, Adam Jones, and R. C. Lee. Photo courtesy of Pioneers' Museum

William S. Jackson was a prominent man of affairs in the new town. William Jackson Palmer had asked him to come be the secretary-treasurer of the Denver and Rio Grande Railroad. In 1873, upon dissolution of the William B. Young Bank, Mr. Jackson, C. H. White, and J. H. Barlow bought its safe and fixtures and established in its same building the El Paso County Bank. Mr. Jackson was president and cashier. In 1917 it merged with the First National Bank. This photo shows Mr. Jackson, who had become a widower, with his children. Photo courtesy of Helen Jackson

Colorado Springs was once the haunt of one of Hollywood's favorite monsters, the Phantom of the Opera. The role was made famous by Lon Chaney, Sr. who was born in Colorado Springs on 1 April 1883 to deaf-mute parents. The "man of many faces" undoubtedly learned his great ability at pantomime from communicating with them.

Along with his older brother, John, Chaney wrote his first play, The Little Tycoon. They rented the opera house and it was there that Chaney made his first appearance in his own play. Photo courtesy of Jim Bates

83

It was on the hillside above Seven Falls where Helen Hunt Jackson was buried in 1885. The falls drop nearly 300 feet and are now a privately owned tourist attraction. Photo from authors' collection

William Wagner was the choice of the citizens for their first mayor. He served two terms (1876-1877) and was always prominent in the work of the Colorado Springs Company. He served under General William J. Palmer during the Civil War and became a major in the 15th Pennsylvania Cavalry. Photo from authors' collection

The Peak greets the dawn of the day, and lifts a gilded finger of rock to salute the setting sun, and under the touch of the whirlwind makes sweet music on a granite harp. It is Colorado's gift. There it stands and will stand after all funeral flowers fade, after our own dirge is sung by others; long after these tenements of clay, mortal man and all his works have perished. It will stand until the heavens are no more and the mountains melt under the feet of the great Jehovah.

Helen Hunt came to the Pikes Peak region in 1873 and immediately fell in love with it. After two years of enjoying the mountains and their magnetic influence upon her pen, she married William S. Jackson. Her fame is international as a poet, and her writings, Ramona, Nellie's Silver Mine, Bits of Travel, and Bits of Talk, are brilliantly written. She died suddenly of cancer in 1885 and was buried above Seven Falls on the Hull Family property. In 1891 Mrs. Hull began charging admission—an enterprise comparable to exhibiting Siamese twins. William Jackson's attempt to purchase the property was unsuccessful, and in 1891 Helen Hunt Jackson's remains were moved to Evergreen Cemetery. Photo courtesy of Pioneers' Museum

Thomas Nast, famous Harper's Weekly artist, drew this cartoon on the stage of the Colorado Springs Opera House in 1887. It signifies his opinion of the misnaming of Colorado Springs. He thought that the name had as much use for the word "springs" as a bucking bronco would have for a spring. The original hangs in Pioneers' Museum. Photo courtesy of Pioneers' Museum

The Great Muldoon fraud in 1879 was to prove "the missing link." Made of animal products and clay then fired in a kiln, it possessed a three-inch tail. This brainstorm of P. T. Barnum was planted and then excavated south of Colorado Springs and caused a great sensation throughout the world. Later the hoax was revealed by an employee who claimed he was not getting his share of the gate receipts. Photo from authors' collection

The Pikes Peak Carriage Road was opened in 1889 by John Hundley, an enterprising young man and owner of a Colorado Springs livery stable. In the early morning, visitors to Pikes Peak would take the Midland Railroad to Cascade, where they disembarked. From there they rode in four-mule surreys to the summit of the mountain and back down, all in a single day. The cost was $2.50 per person. Photo from authors' collection

Mrs. Virginia McClurg arrived in Colorado Springs in 1877. She became chief of staff of the Evening Telegraph newspaper and lectured on equal suffrage over the state.

In 1882 she was the first white woman to visit the Indian ruins of Mesa Verde in southwestern Colorado and to write about them in eastern and western journals. Mrs. McClurg was instrumental in Mesa Verde becoming a national monument. Photo from authors' collection

The Pikes Peak Cog Railroad was started by David H. Moffatt in 1889 and completed by Zalmon G. Simmons in 1890. The first cars reached the summit of the peak on 30 June 1890. This photograph was taken almost exactly one year later. Photo courtesy of Pioneers' Museum

1891~1900

7 CHAPTER 1891~1900

Colorado Springs doubled in size after the discovery of gold in the region. One of the most colorful epics in American history began when Robert Womack ambled down from the hills where he was running cattle with a specimen of gold-bearing ore. At first people were doubtful but not Womack or Dr. J. P. Grannis. They returned to the site of the discovery and staked a claim. That fall a mining camp sprang up and was named for a small stream in the area, Cripple Creek. By spring the gold rush was on; people poured in by the thousands; gold mills and railroads were built and the peaceful little community at the foot of Pikes Peak became a boom town. Bonanza kings invested their wealth in Colorado Springs and built elaborate mansions in the north end of town. Wood Avenue was known as Millionaire's Row.

A few streets down from Millionaire's Row was Dead Man's Row, named for the health seekers who continued to arrive because of the extolled benefits of the high altitude and dry climate.

The city never lacked rich patrons wanting to contribute materially toward the continuing growth. Between 1890 and 1900 the population increased from about 11,000 to 23,000 citizens.

The prosperity and economic growth continued until World War I intervened and changed the direction of history internationally as well as locally.

Bob Womack built a cabin on the old Levi Welty ranch on Cripple Creek which had been acquired by his brother William. He named it Poverty Gulch and during his cattle-tending chores he kept a lookout for signs of gold. When he found gold-bearing ore in 1878, he started a search for its source where he believed there would be a rich deposit of gold. He was right. Womack staked his first claim in 1886 and his second in 1890. This was called the El Paso lode.

Womack later sold his claim for $500 and died penniless in Colorado Springs in 1909. Photo from authors' collection

In 1890, Mrs. Anne E. Harding bought a small acreage of land in Cheyenne Canyon and erected a high tent with the intention of keeping "paying guests." Her venture was successful and in a few years she had a permanent structure built. Her profits mounted and Camp Harding became a year-round business. The building was at first just a single floor, but the popularity of the camp forced the addition of two more floors. Camp Harding, opposite the intersection of Cheyenne Road and Highland, still exists virtually unchanged and is operated as an apartment house. Photo from authors' collection

This is a view of Victor, Colorado as it looked in 1900. While Cripple Creek earned most of the fame from the rich goldfields and mines, all but two of the successful mines were in Victor. Although the town was not as successful in gold fame as its rival, it was the home of broadcaster Lowell Thomas. Photo courtesy of Pioneers' Museum

Winfield Scott Stratton, a Colorado Springs carpenter, became the first Cripple Creek gold millionaire. He sold the Independence Mine for $10 million and distributed much of his fortune locally. He felt "wealth should be used to develop the region from whence it came." He lived alone. At his death on 14 September 1902, thirteen women claimed to be his widow; only one was acknowledged. Photo courtesy of Pioneers' Museum

The Cripple Creek area didn't amount to anything as a mining district until Jimmie Burns and Jimmie Doyle, Colorado Springs firemen, and Winfield Scott Stratton, a Colorado Springs carpenter and cabinet-maker, got interested and established their

Portland and Independence claims.
    This picture shows Bob Womack's developed mining claim in Poverty Gulch, Cripple Creek, Victor District, 1901. Photo from authors' collection

Shredded Wheat originated in Colorado Springs on the Kiowa Street side of the Hagerman building, the shaded side of this photo. This is an account from the Colorado Springs Gazette, 23 March 1894:

"The Colorado Springs Cereal Food Company started their plant in the Hagerman Block. The cereal food is made from choice Colorado wheat and is formed into a small bread shaped loaf or eaten as a shredded breakfast dish. Mr. Andrew Sagendorf is the manager and proposes to give the citizens an opportunity to try the product."

The company operated in Colorado Springs for two years then moved to Denver. Later it moved to Niagara Falls, New York. Shredded Wheat is now a Nabisco product. Photo from authors' collection

Some visitors wished to spend more time on Pikes Peak than the Hundley Tour provided, and this prompted several halfway houses such as this one to be built. Excursions on Pikes Peak were very popular in the 1890s, and anybody who was somebody in Colorado made the visit. Photo courtesy of Pioneers' Museum

392. HALF WAY HOUSE
PIKES PEAK CARRIAGE

It was a view such as this one which inspired Katherine Lee Bates to write America the Beautiful. *Miss Bates, a professor of English at Wellesley College, came to Colorado Springs to lecture at summer school classes conducted by Colorado College in 1893. Photo from authors' collection*

Among the thousands of carriage alpinists to scale Pikes Peak in the 1890 decade was Katherine Lee Bates, who made the journey during the summer of 1893. At the summit she wrote. ''The opening lines of the hymn floated into my mind as I was looking out over the sealike expanse of fertile country spreading away so far under those ample skies.'' On this spot she began to write America the Beautiful, *and finished it in Colorado Springs. Photo courtesy of Pioneers' Museum*

In 1893 artist Charles Craig, called "Pink Face Charley" by the Indians who posed for him, originated the fashion among the Ute braves of wearing a single feather as headdress. He relates that a young buck, wearing three feathers in his sombrero, came for a sitting. Craig asked him to remove the feathers then thrust one in the Indian's plaited hair, standing it upright. This style remained in vogue among the Indians long afterward. Drawing by Charles Craig; from Pioneers' Museum Collection

During the tense period in the gold fields, Mr. Tom Parrish and Mr. D. V. Donaldson turned their attention to the flower fields. In 1893 they launched a Flower Parade. People with equipages of one sort or another covered them with flowers and paraded the streets. This became a yearly festival, each time more elaborate. The Flower Parades were replaced in 1912 by the Shan Kive, a street fair and carnival. In 1936 the Pikes Peak or Bust Rodeo celebration replaced the Shan Kive. Photo courtesy of Pioneers' Museum

Miss Bessie Henry's private school, called the Kinnikinnik, was opened in 1893 on the southwest corner of the Colorado College Campus. In 1899 the Misses Scarborough, Howard, and Henry, offered kindergarten, primary, and advanced courses. This picture shows the cooking class of 1904. The school changed ownership several times. In 1930, under the ownership of Mrs. Robert K. Potter, it became the San Luis school and moved to the Austin Bluffs area operating as a boarding school for upper class girls. It ceased operating several years later. Photo courtesy of Pioneers' Museum

Early Colorado Springs residents erected Totman Patent Houses, known as Chicago Houses. Spring Byington was born in one of these houses in Colorado Springs in 1893. The picture shows Mount Lincoln and Mount Washington in the background. Photo courtesy of Pioneers' Museum

Dr. James A. Hart delivered most of the babies in Colorado Springs in the 1890s and early 1900s. He is pictured in the reading room of the El Paso Club.

The statue (left) is Mrs. Pomeroy, named for its bachelor purchaser, James P. Pomeroy. Photo from authors' collection

Andy Adams was a famous writer of western stories who participated in many of the great cattle drives of steers to the shipping centers. Here he wrote many of his stories in the rough. Among them are: The Log of a Cowboy; Reed Anthony, Cowman, and The Ranch On the Beaver.

Andy Adams came to Colorado Springs in 1892 and did some writing here, but mainly he acted as a broker in the mining exchange. Photo from authors' collection

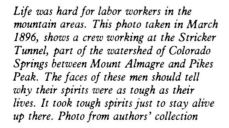

Life was hard for labor workers in the mountain areas. This photo taken in March 1896, shows a crew working at the Stricker Tunnel, part of the watershed of Colorado Springs between Mount Almagre and Pikes Peak. The faces of these men should tell why their spirits were as tough as their lives. It took tough spirits just to stay alive up there. Photo from authors' collection

Hiawatha Gardens, built in the 1890s, was damaged twice by fire, once before World War I, when it was owned by Hal Leddy and again in 1920, when it was owned by Eli Gross.

In the earlier years Hiawatha Gardens was the social center of Manitou. Summer visitors came here by train and stayed most of the season. The Gardens was their main entertainment center.

The ballroom had its veranda facing west and on moonlit nights the outline of the mountains added a special charm and enchantment. It is now the House of Prime Rib. Photo courtesy of Pioneers' Museum

Entertainment in and around Colorado Springs was easy to find before television. The adventuresome could always satisfy their search with a trip up the rickety Mount Manitou (sometimes incorrectly known as Red Mountain) Incline. The cars worked by a pulley system, with each car serving as the weight. As one descended, it pulled the other car up. If the cable snapped, guides assured the riders that two big springs at the bottom would stop the plunge—Manitou Springs and Colorado Springs. Photo courtesy of Pioneers' Museum

101

Mrs. Mamie Wilson drove her horse, Prince, and a canvas-covered buggy from Carthage, Missouri, to Colorado Springs in 1897, with her young son and daughter and a pug dog. She took in sewing to support her family and had a good trade from the Broadmoor ladies who paid well for fancy dresses and suits.

This photo was taken at the Balanced Rock and Steamship Rock in the Garden of the Gods. Photo courtesy of Pioneers' Museum

Wyman's Second Hand Store and Auction House was located at 10 South Tejon Street in 1896. Mr. Wyman is standing in the center and Mrs. Nellie Rouse is the lady seated. Photo courtesy of Pioneers' Museum

The Colorado Springs Sun, *a weekly newspaper primarily for the black population of Colorado Springs, was published in 1898 and 1899. J. M. Booker was editor, W. H. Duncan, city editor, and W. E. King, business manager. Photo from authors' collection*

These are the "Dirty Dozen" of Company M, who fought for the United States during the Spanish-American War in 1898. Photo from authors' collection

Accounts of the first Antlers Hotel fire in 1898 are always interesting but they are made doubly so when sidelights are revealed.

Helen Jackson, the girl in this picture, tells the story: "We children were naturally curious and excited with all the confusion caused by the great fire. Papa would not allow us to go beyond North Park, now Acacia Park. We were all terribly fightened of the high winds blowing great billows of smoke our way. Brother William had the brilliant idea of placing wet sponges under our hats. So there we stood in North Park, dripping in our own little puddles."

William grew up to be Justice of the Supreme Court and Helen became a schoolteacher. Photo courtesy of Pioneers' Museum

In May 1899, the El Paso County Commissioners purchased the 525-acre Liebig Ranch, west of Colorado Springs, along the drainage of Bear Creek. A fireproof brick building was constructed on the farm with money from water rights sales and insurance after the original farm house burned to the ground. Known as the El Paso County Farm now, the building is used for the extremely impoverished people as a shelter, but its future is questionable. The land around it is mostly undeveloped, though parts are used for community gardens.

This photo shows the El Paso County Commissioners and guests at the dedication of the farm, 10 October 1900. Photo from authors' collection

James Bo Fun Da, known as China Jim, opened his second art shop at 7 East Pikes Peak Avenue in 1899. The heavy scent of sandalwood floated out when the windsong-chimed door was opened.

China Jim had a great influence on Oriental decor in many early Colorado Springs homes. Photo from authors' collection

In 1899 John Jacob Astor gave the electrical genius, Nikola Tesla, father of alternating current, $30,000 to conduct electrical experiments in Colorado Springs. Tesla built a laboratory in a cow pasture east of the city and proceeded to prove that the earth was electrically charged, paving the way for the modern electrical power era of today. Photo courtesy of Pioneers' Museum

Winfield Scott Stratton purchased the old street railway system in Colorado Springs on 24 August 1900 and modernized it at an expense to himself of approximately $2 million.

This streetcar descending the South Tejon Street hill was on the Broadmoor, Cheyenne Canon line.

On 1 May 1932, the streetcar service was replaced by that of the Colorado Springs Bus Company. Photo from authors' collection

In 1900 W. S. Stratton purchased twenty acres of the Dixon Ranch at the junction of North and South Cheyenne creeks. He landscaped extensively and built gardens, ponds, swings and amusements rides, and a lavish bandstand, thus transforming the glen into the highly popular Stratton Park. It was opened on 6 June 1901, dedicated by officers of Local 515, Carpenters and Joiners of America. Photo from authors' collection

Mrs. E. B. Simmons is shown sitting on a waterwheel at the site of Bert Meyers Broom Works on the present Cresta Road and Cheyenne Creek. This area is now residential. Photo from authors' collection

On 26 November 1900, the most dreadful wind Colorado Springs ever experienced began. The Big Blow removed roofs from even large buildings and flattened large trees. The government signal station recorded eighty m.p.h. winds until friction burned off the gauge. Photo courtesy of Gazette Telegraph

Stratton's streetcars ran everywhere in town, including to Stratton Park. The olive-green cars were powered by forty horsepower Corliss motors and were wonderful, elegant, five-cent rides.

The bandstand was the Sunday home of the Colorado Midland Band which performed here every summer. Unfortunately most of the park was destroyed in the floods of 1921 and 1935. Photo courtesy of Pioneers' Museum

Tourism, Tuberculosis and the Turn of the Century

8 CHAPTER 1901~1920

The turn of the century in Colorado Springs brought many changes to the city. Some of its businessmen became millionaires from Cripple Creek (actually Victor) gold. Some of them spent a lot of money on civic causes. The lure of gold swelled the population from 21,000 to 30,000 during the period from 1901 to 1910, but it was Cripple Creek and Victor that were the "big cities" of the Pikes Peak region, and each was much larger than Colorado Springs. The mortality rate in the city was exceptionally high, but statistics do not always illustrate the truth. The climate here was considered ideal for people who suffered from tuberculosis. Thousands came here to breathe the crisp, dry, mold-free air, but many came too late and died anyway. Sanatoria were established for tuberculosis recovery. The influence was also felt upon architecture as many houses were built with numerous, large, open-air porches for sitting. From 1910 to 1920, the production cost of gold rose and diminished the prospects of wealth, even in illusion, and with the expected high mortality rate, though many continued to come to the city, its population increased by just 100 people each year after 1910.

North Cheyenne Canyon Park was a popular outing place for the residents of Colorado Springs after 1900. People would hike or ride to Bruin Inn and dine on fresh mountain trout, entertained by the Bruin Inn Novelty Orchestra. Professors Tenney, Strieby, and Loud from Colorado College among others built summer cabins in the canyon above Helen Hunt Falls. This photo shows the pavilion and carriage route near the current Fort Carson Rock Climbing Demonstration Area about 1915. Photo from authors' collection

In June 1901 the Short Line to Cripple Creek Railroad was opened as an economic means of hauling ore from the gold fields to Colorado Springs. The route was begun by the first president of the line, Irving Howbert, when freight rates of the Colorado Midland Railroad became prohibitively costly. Originally intended strictly for the shipment of ore, the route became very popular with sightseers. President Theodore Roosevelt took the trip and afterward called it "the trip that bankrupts the English language."

In 1923 after the gold standard was adopted and Cripple Creek went down, the railroad was closed. This picture is of the dedication and the first running of the train in June 1901. Photo from authors' collection

While the Colorado Midland Railroad was in operation, some very popular outings were the wildflower trains during mid-summer. Due to the short growing season, many of the alpine plants bloom at the same time, and the spectacle is unmatched anyplace else. Many notable botanists have come here to study the flora, beginning with Dr. Edwin James who made the first recorded ascent of Pikes Peak on 20 June 1820 with the Fremont Exploration. The book, Rocky Mountain Wildflowers by Dr. Frederic Clements and Dr. Edith Clements was written from studies at the Pikes Peak Alpine Laboratory, near Minnehaha, and is considered by many to be the finest book written on this subject. The Colorado Springs Firemans' Band went along on this excursion to provide entertainment. Photo courtesy of Pioneers' Museum

Dr. J. Bidmead Wright and Wilbur Rice set out for Denver in this Locomobile in 1901 at 11:00 a.m. They arrived in Denver at 10:00 p.m. The Locomobile was shipped to Dr. Wright from Massachusetts in several packing boxes and was assembled by him in 1900. Photo from authors' collection

In 1901 the name Nordrach Ranch was given to this sanatorium for tubercular patients since the proposed method of treatment was to be much the same as first introduced in the Black Forest of Germany by Dr. Nordrach. The treatment consisted of many hours in the open air, suitable food at regular hours and light exercise. Great emphasis was placed on the contentment and happiness of the patients. The sanatorium ceased operation around 1913. Photo courtesy of Pioneers' Museum

St. Francis Hospital started as the Colorado Midland Railroad Hospital in 1887, with Dr. B. P. Anderson in charge and the Sisterhood of St. Francis of Perpetual Adoration as staff. When the building on East Pikes Peak Avenue was opened in 1888, the Midland patients were moved there.

Several additions and renovations have taken place at the hospital at this location. Photo from authors' collection

Dr. Edwin S. Solly was an early arrival here. In his belief, this was the most favored place in the world to build an institution for the treatment of tubercular patients. In January 1902 General William J. Palmer announced he would give 100 acres of land and $50,000 for the construction of suitable buildings. The name of the institution became Cragmor.

The buildings are now part of the University of Colorado, Colorado Springs campus. Photo courtesy of Pioneers' Museum

The Ambler Ranch of 1,000 acres was purchased in 1908 for $15,000 by the Modern Woodmen of America to build their tuberculosis sanatorium. It opened 1 January 1909 and was a self-contained city in itself with 220 separate buildings. The sanatorium closed in the 1940s. Since 1954 the buildings have been occupied by the Sisters of St. Francis of Perpetual Adoration. Photo from authors' collection

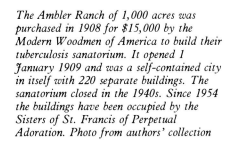

Tuberculosis patients are shown convalescing in the fresh air and snow outside the Gardiner tents at Modern Woodmen of America Sanatorium. Photo from authors' collection

Massive frame homes with open air sleeping porches were built in the 1900s for tuberculosis convalescents. Photo from authors' collection

An account in the Colorado Springs Gazette, *31 January 1904 states: "In reviewing the work done by New York Doctors since they first opened their offices in the city, we see nothing but success stamped on every effort. New York Doctors have one of the best equipped offices in the city, occupying the second floor of the Post Office building 120 East Pikes Peak Avenue."*

The New York Doctors' method of operation was to diagnose and treat free, charging only for the prescribed medicine. This photograph was taken in 1915. Photo from authors' collection

These are the student nurses who were working at Bellevue Sanatorium, later named Colorado Conference Deaconess Hospital, in 1907. Members of the group are: Sarah Bradshaw (1907 graduate), Nellie M. Joyce, Mable Blomberg, Emma I. Absher, Clemmie Irwin (1909 graduate), Miss Kehoe (Superintendent of Nurses), Miss Cummings, Miss Anderson, and Miss Davis. Photo from authors' collection

Bethel Hospital, formerly called Colorado Conference Deaconess Hospital, was dedicated and opened on July 2, 1911. Bethel Sanatorium (not pictured), opened in 1926 as the National Episcopal Sanatorium for Tuberculosis, was Methodist operated and stood where the National Sports Building is today.

Memorial Hospital, named in 1943 for those who lost their lives in World War II and operated by the city of Colorado Springs, was built around the old Bethel Hospital and was renovated during the 1970s. Photo from authors' collection

This aerial photograph of Penrose Hospital was taken in 1925 before the twelve-story addition was built. The original Glockner Sanatorium is shown toward the bottom of the picture, with the Glockner Penrose addition in the center. Photo from authors' collection

Getting Supper in the Rockies. An enterprising photographer dreamed up this set in the early 1900s. Many families became snap-of-the-shutter, covered wagon travelers. Note the house above the woman's head. Photo courtesy of Pioneers' Museum

GETTING SUPPER IN THE ROCKIES.

"Mount Cutler Crime Solved by Identification of Teeth," reported the Colorado Springs Gazette in 1904. "The body of a woman was found on Mount Cutler between North and South Cheyenne canyons. The unidentified victim was buried in Evergreen Cemetery, but not before some members of the police department had the idea of saving her teeth in hopes that she could later be identified by them. It was not long after the pictures had been publicized, that the newspaper published the news with the headline: 'Denver physician recognized teeth—Express opinion after close inspection that murdered woman and Mrs. Bessie Bouton are one and the same.'" Drawing courtesy of Colorado Springs Police Department

Milton Franklin Andrew confessed to the murder of Mrs. Bessie Bouton and committed suicide in December 1904. Drawing courtesy of Colorado Springs Police Department

Captain Ellen E. Jack set up a few rental cabins and a curio shop for tourists on the High Drive above Bear Creek Canyon. She was a loveable local character in the 1900s. Photo from authors' collection

The El Paso County Courthouse, designed by August J. Smith, was completed and presented to the taxpayers on 18 May 1903. It was built on land donated by the Colorado Springs Company.

From 1909 to 1933 the El Paso County Pioneers' Association set up exhibits of pioneer relics in the Courthouse hallways. Seen on the sidewalk in this picture is Mrs. Maud McFarran Price, lifetime curator of the relics.

On 29 September 1972 the building was entered in the National Register of Historic Places. On 4 June 1973, the El Paso County Commissioners handed the deed to the Courthouse and Alamo Square to the Mayor of Colorado Springs who in turn handed the same documents to the chairman of the Pioneers' Museum Board. The original relics plus thousands more are housed in the old Courthouse, now the Pioneers' Museum. Photo from authors' collection

The "Watermellon" was a ride at Stratton Park playground about 1915. Stratton Park opened in the early 1900s in the 1,500 to 2,000 blocks on West Cheyenne Road. It closed after a flood in 1921 and now is the property of the P. E. O. Organization. Photo from authors' collection

Palmer Park was a gift to the city in 1907 from General William Jackson Palmer. The sandstone bluffs which overlook the city and Pikes Peak are threaded by trails to idyllic spots and overlooks, all planned and built by Palmer. In an 1869 letter to his wife, "Queen," he wrote that the great herds of bison which he saw on the prairie would become extinct unless they were protected. His foresight allowed for the 100-foot-wide streets in the downtown area (to accommodate our automobiles) and for our city-mountain parks which today preserve the wilderness and solitude for the residents of Colorado Springs for generations to come. Photo from authors' collection

This is a picture of the second house at Glen Eyrie, built in 1903-1905. It was partly razed and the Tudor mansion was constructed. Photo from authors' collection

The most magnificent home ever built in the Pikes Peak region is Glen Eyrie, the fabulous estate of General William Jackson Palmer in Queens Canyon, just north of the Garden of the Gods. His manor house and satellite buildings are located in the midst of 225 acres of crags, canyons, and meadows. Original bills kept by General Palmer show he spent more than a million dollars in making his estate into a place of beauty, stateliness, and luxury. The manor house was completed in 1905, but even up to the time of Palmer's death in 1909 he was still planning construction and improvements.

The buildings are now owned and operated by the Navigators, and used for religious conferences and training. Photo from authors' collection

The Charter Convention was elected on 19 January 1909 to draw up a charter for the city of Colorado Springs. Members shown here are: William M. Banning, Jacob Bishoff, Willard N. Burgess, Frank F. Castello, William J. Chinn, James E. Eubanks, Thomas J. Fisher, Joseph B. Fowler, Moses C. Gile, Oliver B. Grimes, Henry C. Hall, John M. Harnan, Henry W. Hoagland, P. M. Kistler, Horace G. Lunt, Thomas McCaffery, Myer S. Rafield, Harry H. Seldomridge, Edward C. Sharer, William H. Spurgeon, and Edgar J. Ellrich. Photo courtesy of Pioneers' Museum

Reunion of the 15th Pennsylvania Cavalry at Glen Eyrie on August 1907. General William Jackson Palmer, a Pennsylvania Quaker, felt strongly that men of all races and creeds deserved to be free men. So thinking, he organized a cavalry troop among his friends, served with distinction during the Civil War, and was made a brevet brigadier general at a very early age. At the reunion General Palmer said: "I feel sure that no war of aggression or for spread of the empire would have drawn these men from their homes. It was a cause for which they fought. I am proud to have commanded and to have since retained the respect of such a body of men goes without saying." Photo courtesy of Pioneers' Museum

Julie McMillan, formerly Julie Villiers Lewis, came to Colorado Springs with her first husband, Jim McMillan, who was suffering from tuberculosis. On 11 January 1901, she attended a clambake hosted by Spencer Penrose. A few months after this, Jim McMillan died from his illness. Not intending to follow the tragic story of her widowed friend Edith Field who vowed not to remarry, Julie turned her attention toward finding a new husband, a process which consumed all of five minutes. On 26 April 1906 her snaring efforts paid off as she and Spencer Penrose were married at St. George's Church in London.

Spencer Penrose, known by his friends as ''Spec,'' was one of the three most influential persons ever to live in Colorado Springs. He was born on 2 November 1865 to a noteworthy Philadelphia family, and came to the Pikes Peak region in 1892. Lured by the gold fields around Cripple Creek, he began his plan to earn great wealth along with his hometown friend, Charley Tutt. While he was somewhat successful in Cripple Creek, it was another strategic metal that mushroomed the Penrose bank account. Spec amassed his fortune from a 1903 investment in Utah copper, in behalf of a revolutionary metal extracting method developed by geologist Daniel C. Jackling. This investment made

Spec's family very wealthy, and his fortune was put to use improving the quality of life in the Pikes Peak region. Spec's interest in this city was felt in every corner and most subtle nuance. He built the Broadmoor, the Pikes Peak and Cheyenne Mountain Auto Highways, the Cheyenne Mountain Zoo. He started the El Pomar Foundation, the Pikes Peak Hill Climb, the Penrose Tumor Clinic. The list of his accomplishments in the Pikes Peak region consumes volumes of literature. He died on 7 December 1939, but his big-hearted gifts to the community are still active and a reminder that generosity and wealth are a rare and extremely fortunate combination. Photo courtesy of Pioneers' Museum

Julie Penrose was as much involved in the dynamic new projects of the region as her husband. Together they built the Monument Valley Municipal Swimming Pool in Palmer's Monument Valley Park. In 1919 she had a pastoral Catholic church built in the Broadmoor and named it for her granddaughter Pauline. That same year she started the Broadmoor Art Academy, a culmination of effort in Julie's lifelong love of the arts and their study. Before her death in 1956 she gave $5 million of El Pomar money to build Penrose Hospital on the site of the old Glockner Hospital of North Cascade Avenue. El Pomar continues in the tradition of funding needy and great humanitarian causes. Photo courtesy of Pioneers' Museum

The heirs of Charles W. Perkins, owner of the Garden of the Gods property, at Perkins' request, donated it to three trustees, Messrs. H. C. Hall, H. LeB. Wills, and D. V. Donaldson, with instructions to deed it to the city of Colorado Springs, before 1 January 1911. A bronze tablet on the right gateway rock wall celebrates this generous gift. Photo from authors' collection

Indians were an important part of tourism in Colorado Springs. This photo was taken at the Hidden Inn, Garden of the Gods in 1910. Photo from authors' collection

"Bath House John" Coughlin started the old zoo in Ivywild in 1906. He financed the Zoological Park until 1918 when it was converted into one of the first automobile campgrounds in the Pikes Peak region. The land was originally homesteaded by John Wolfe in 1860. Photo courtesy of Pioneers' Museum

Zoological Park featured a sacred cow, several bears, eagles, camels, bison, and other animals. Several of the streets in the residential area which replaced the zoo were named for the animals, and they exist today as connecting streets between Cheyenne Road and Cheyenne Boulevard, near Eighth Street. Photo courtesy of Pioneers' Museum

Among the animals at Zoological Park, were several amusements including a miniature railroad, a circle swing, a cane rack, a roller skating rink, a merry-go-round, a penny arcade, the old mill which included a gondola trip, and the roller coaster shown here. Photo courtesy of Pioneers' Museum

This is Nelson's Camp, a rest stop camp built by Frank Nelson in 1908. He was a caretaker and runoff inspector for the city of Colorado Springs. Nelson's Camp was located on Cheyenne Creek at the 9,900 foot level of Almagre Mountain. When time permitted, Mr. Nelson prospected but was never very successful. In 1925 he named one gold digging the Lion's Claim because there were puma tracks nearby in the snow. Photo courtesy of Pioneers' Museum

At the home of Professor M. C. Gile in May 1905, a group of thirty-five men and women met to organize a mountain climbing and outing club. During the 22 May meeting the new name, Pikes Peak Climbing Club, was adopted. The knowledge of the geography acquired by the club's experience was compiled into the first Pikes Peak Atlas *by member Robert Ormes and was published by the Chamber of Commerce in 1913. Now known as the Saturday Knights, the members hike on every Saturday through the year, regardless of inclement weather. In the evening after the trip they settle the affairs of the world in a cheerful campfire gathering. Photo courtesy of Pioneers' Museum*

Tacky parties were popular in the 1900s. This one was held at the Giddings residence, 222 E. Uintah Street. Photo from authors' collection

This Christmas party was held at the home of Mr. and Mrs. William O'Brien, 1210 Wood Avenue, in 1912.

Identified are: Margaret Giddings, Bill Hunt, Therusha La Mercier, Charles Walker Wright, Grace Bartlett, Herbert Hunt, Beverly Wright McHugh, Margaret "Muff" O'Brien, Junior Burns, Artie Friedman, Ralph Giddings, and Martha Lowe.

"Muff," the prima donna in the photo, became a ballerina. Photo courtesy of Pioneers' Museum

The Cooking Club was created by Spencer Penrose in 1912. At this time the gentlemen epicureans met in the homes of the members. Penrose then provided a site on Cheyenne Mountain and a functional building where he presided over his company gourmets. It is still in existence. Photo from authors' collection

One of the "Mile a Minute" scooters is shown descending the Cog Railroad from Pikes Peak, above the Halfway House switch. In October 1911 George DeWalt was killed when he was thrown from such a toboggan. Riders who braved the more than fifty mph speeds did so at their own risk. Photo from authors' collection

On 17 July 1913 this twenty horsepower Buick Bearcat, with passengers W. W. Brown and J. R. Bradley, was the third recorded automobile to reach the summit of Pikes Peak. The ascent took five hours, thirty-five minutes from Colorado Springs. Even today's marathon runners can beat that time. Photo courtesy of Pioneers' Museum

The big snowstorm of 1913 paralyzed the city of Colorado Springs. Nearly four feet of heavy, wet snow was recorded. This is how Pikes Peak Avenue looked the day after, when the storm was clearing. Photo courtesy of Pioneers' Museum

In 1897 Henry R. Wray, Dr. S. L. Caldwell, Dr. S.E. Solly, Dr. E. F. Gildea, and professors Frances Walker and H. E. Worden organized the Town and Gown Golf Club, the third golf club organized in the United States. The clubhouse was a residence in the 1100 block of North Wahsatch, and links were built in the prairie near North Junior High. W. K. Jewett, vice-president of the Colorado Springs National Bank was the most influential member. In 1919 he acquired all the stock of the Suburban Land and Water Company and offered the property as a gift under certain conditions to the city. On 25 June 1919 the city council accepted, and the property became the Patty Stewart Jewett Memorial Golf Club, named for his wife, an avid golf and sports enthusiast. Photo courtesy of Pioneers' Museum

131

After the Day Nursery was started in 16 March 1897 and had operated at several different locations, Mrs. F. M. P. Taylor announced she would provide $160,000 dollars for a new building to be built on land purchased from Mr. Asa T. Jones on South Tejon and Rio Grande streets. It was opened on 20 December 1923, with forty children enrolled.

This 1940 picture shows part of the magnificent building designed by architect William Stickney. The Day Nursery has an enrollment today of more than eighty children. Photo from authors' collection

This picture of Colorado Springs was taken from the tower of the El Paso County Courthouse in 1912. The famous Peck's Corral, started by John W. Peck in 1903, can be seen in the lower center. Originally it was entered from Cucharras Street and was back of the real estate office of James H. Bruce, father of former Police Chief, I. B. Bruce.

Farmers from all directions put up their horses at Peck's Corral and many would pass the night sleeping in their wagons. There was so much activity with trading and selling that a turntable was constructed for handy turning of the wagons. At one time a merry-go-round was operated for the amusement of farm children while their parents went about their business. The site is now owned by the city of Colorado Springs and serves as a parking lot. Photo courtesy of Penrose Library

Dr. Caroline Spencer, representing the Civic League of Colorado Springs, presented a plan for a city flag to the city council in July 1912. The legend of the adopted flag is this: The white field represents the cleanliness and health of the city; the blue border our blue skies; the shield carries the sun; the mountain stands for Pikes Peak; the gold ingots our mining industry and a green band about the shield represents the park system.

Photo shows former Mayor Harry Hoth and Chuck Heitman inspecting the flag, now stored at city hall. Photo from authors' collection

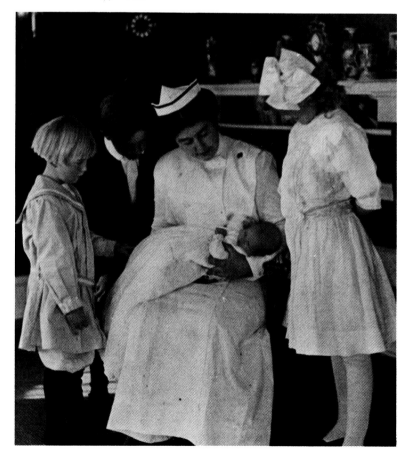

On 28-29 August 1912, the Big Balloon Race was launched from Washburn Field of Colorado College. John Watts, pilot of Kansas City II, was the winner, floating forty-two miles north before he landed near Castle Rock. Communication with the balloon was not possible, and when it disappeared to the north the whereabouts of the craft and safety of its pilot became a national news item. Photo courtesy of Pioneers' Museum

These are the children of Mr. and Mrs. John William Ryter, pioneer Colorado Springs residents, in their home in Broadmoor on 16 December 1913: Julius William, Lawrence J., Nurse McKay, Ruth M. and baby Agnes. Photo courtesy of Pioneers' Museum

By the terms of the will of Winfield Scott Stratton, the major portion of his estate was to be used in the erection and endowment of an institution to be known as the Myron Stratton Home, as a memorial to his father. Its inhabitants were to be "those who are by youth, sickness, or other infirmity unable to earn a livelihood." The Myron Stratton Home opened in March 1914. It is still in operation and additional programs are anticipated. Photo from authors' collection

Sinton Dairy float was part of the Labor Day parade in 1914. The Temple Theater is in the background. This site on Nevada Avenue is now occupied by the Colorado Springs National Drive-In Bank. Photo from authors' collection

The entrance to the new Pikes Peak Highway. The construction of this second highest road in the United States was begun in 1915 and completed in June 1916. Built at a cost of $350,000, it was a toll road operated by the Pikes Peak Automobile Company until 1936 when it became a free transportation system. In 1948, because of the great expense of maintaining a road at this high elevation, it was necessary to re-establish the toll. Currently the road is owned and operated by the city of Colorado Springs. Photo courtesy of Pioneers' Museum

At the Manitou Mineral Water Company, the stinky seltzer-water was bottled and sold much as the European mineral waters are today. They were supposed to cure everything and were praised most highly by the doctors who had invested in the enterprise. However, this business failed as have all others at this location; an Indian curse is supposed to be responsible. This is how the company looked in 1915. Photo courtesy of Pioneers' Museum

The Corley Coal Company yard was located on East Costilla Street at the Santa Fe Railroad tracks. It was started in 1916 by W. D. Corley who was connected with the Franceville Coal Mines east of the city. The Corley coal interests are now in the coal fields at Florence, Colorado. Pen and ink drawing by John P. Inness; from authors' collection

This eight cylinder Romano was the second-day winner of the first Pikes Peak Hill Climb of 11-12 August 1916. The race was organized by Spencer Penrose, builder of the highway. The elegant Penrose Cup winner's trophy cost $1,200 and was made by Bailey, Banks, and Biddle of Philadelphia. Photo from authors' collection

Alexander Smith Cochran, a New York carpetmaker, purchased the Glen Eyrie estate in 1918.

Cochran and his bride, an aspiring opera singer, didn't relish maintaining a sixty-seven room castle, so they closed it up. On the grounds, they built the Pink House, a plush well-built home with elegant fireplaces. Note the wood burning stove in the fireplace in this picture. Photo courtesy of Pioneers' Museum

On Labor Day 1916 Colorado Springs staged a boxing match between the lightweight champion of the world, Freddie Welsh of Wales, and Charlie White from Chicago. Bleachers were set up in the area of Colorado Avenue and Spruce Street. Before the starting bell, about 500 people had entered one of the bleachers when it began to crackle and sway. There were many injuries and a few fatalities. The fight went on anyway and Welsh won it by the referee's decision, ten rounds to five. Photo courtesy of Pioneers' Museum

In the summer of 1918 the new Broadmoor Hotel opened for business and immediately set a new standard for excellence. Spencer Penrose and his associates were the moving forces behind the hotel, designed by Warren and Wetmore, architects of the Biltmore, Commodore, and Ritz hotels, and Grand Central Station in New York. This 1921 painting by John P. Inness shows the hotel as it looked on a snowy December night. Painting from authors' collection

Mrs. Effie M. Winters-Rothchild poses with her horse, Pretty. She donated the horse for auction to the Red Cross to help raise money during World War I. Mrs.

Spencer Penrose bought the horse for $1,000 then gave the animal back to Mrs. Winters-Rothchild. Photo from authors' collection

The World War I Battery "C" was organized in May 1916. Several Colorado Springs businessmen, urged by the National Security League, met and formed Battery C, 148th Field Artillery.

Father of Battery "C," local lawyer, Victor Hungerford, was elected captain. Photo from authors' collection

Miners from the Pikeview Coal Mine, near current Rockrimmon, ride a bus in the Victory Day parade on 11 November 1918. Photo courtesy of Pioneers' Museum

"VICTORY DAY"
COLO. SPRINGS - NOV. 11 - 1918

The entire population of Colorado Springs, more than 20,000 people, lined Tejon Street for the celebration parade on Victory Day, 1918. This photo looks across the northwest corner of Acacia Park. Photo courtesy of Pioneers' Museum

Between the Wars

9 CHAPTER
1921~1940

With World War I out the way, Colorado Springs again turned toward prosperity. Gold was not so much a factor as its production cost rose to erase the profit margin and most of the great mines were forced to close. Cripple Creek and Victor went down.

But Colorado Springs was already a many-faceted gem of a city, and its future and growth were assured. Then there were the Penroses, marvelously indescribable people! The Depression shut Cripple Creek down further and by the outbreak of World War II it was nearly a ghost town. The population of Cripple Creek declined from more than 30,000 to just a few hundred while the population of Colorado Springs steadily rose from 30,000 to 36,000. Where did Cripple Creek go?

This is Colorado Springs as it looked in about 1920 from the summit of Pikes Peak. The population was 30,105. The brightly lit area right from the photo center and left of the black shadow of Camerons Cone is the original town-site as it was laid out by General William Jackson Palmer. Photo from authors' collection

144

145

In the late teens and early twenties, a restauranteur, George Stokes, opened an eating house on Pikes Peak Avenue, at right in this picture. His main feature was chili and it became so popular that he could not handle the crowds. Later he went into the canning business with his famous chili receipt. It is still one of the most popular chili's on the market today. Photo from authors' collection

The Civic Auditorium was accepted by architects, C. E. Thomas, MacLaren, and Heatherington on 8 July 1923. The distant buildings in the picture are: the Y.W.C.A., the second Antlers Hotel, the Exchange National Bank, and the Mining Exchange building.

The auditorium is used now for sports events, traveling performances, and flea markets. Photo courtesy of city of Colorado Springs.

In the 1920s, before motels and motor homes, tourist auto parks were popular. Many, such as this one, were located close to scenic attractions. Photo from authors' collection

In 1922 Spencer Penrose started a menagerie next to his Broadmoor Hotel. The animals were a priority over the hotel guests and neither complaint of sound or smell moved Spec or his zoo. A lawsuit, however, developed when a child was bitten by a monkey and the parents successfully sought compensation. The zoo was then moved to its present location on Cheyenne Mountain and is one of the world's finest small zoos. Here, Josephine enjoys her after-dinner cigar. Photo courtesy of Pioneers' Museum

A retouched photograph shows the Cheyenne Mountain Highway, built in 1925 by Spencer Penrose. The route was built to draw attention to the Broadmoor and to confound the efforts of Spec's quiet arch-rival, W. D. Corley, to extend another route to the summit of Pikes Peak from his already successful Corley Mountain Highway. Intended for public use and enjoyment, the Cheyenne Mountain Highway was the center for a stormy controversy among residents of the area who did not enjoy the scar upon their mountain. Photo from authors' collection

This is the Recreation Room of the Lodge atop the north summit of Cheyenne Mountain. The Lodge was built in 1925 by Spencer Penrose of the Broadmoor. In July 1926 champion heavyweight Jack Dempsey honeymooned here with his bride, actress Estelle Taylor. The Cheyenne Mountain Highway, which led to the lodge, was a public eyesore for many years since many switchbacks had to be built for the road to ascend the steep east face of the mountain. Penrose, always sensitive to public opinion concerning his enterprises, was particularly hurt by the public outrage over the highway. Photo courtesy of Pioneers' Museum

What began as the Penrose Memorial became the Will Rogers Shrine of the Sun on Cheyenne Mountain. It was built after 1931 for a cost of $250,000 by Spencer Penrose from designs by architect Charles Thomas. Reasonably agreeing that a memorial to himself might be slightly vain, Spec's dilemma was solved when Will Rogers died in a plane crash, and the memorial was named after him. A massive amplification system tolls the daily hours, and in the early evening musical concerts emanate from the system to the backyard delight of anyone living in a five-mile radius of the Shrine. Photo courtesy of Pioneers' Museum

This photo shows the Corley Mountain Highway in early May 1925 above Canyonwood in North Cheyenne Canyon. The devastation from the 1853-1854 fire is still seen in these barren slopes. The heavy runoff from snow and rain caused frequent flooding and erosion damage. Maintenance of the road was a costly, never-ending job. Photo courtesy of Pioneers' Museum

The Corley Mountain Highway at Point Sublime overlooks North Cheyenne Canyon, Mt. Cutler, and Cheyenne Mountain. The road is the free Gold Camp Road today and is a popular but dusty drive from Colorado Springs to Cripple Creek. This is how it looked in 1925. Photo from authors' collection

These are the trestle and first tunnel of the Corley Mountain Highway above North Cheyenne Canyon. Originally this was the route of the Short Line to Cripple Creek, a railroad which opened in June 1901 as an economic method of hauling gold ore from Cripple Creek to Colorado Springs for smelting. In 1923, after the decline of Cripple Creek, the line was closed. The route was purchased by W. D. Corley, who rebuilt it as a motorized mountain highway and opened it in July 1924. Photo from authors' collection

Harry L. Standley, a pioneer photographer of the Pikes Peak region, is responsible for some of the finest scenic mountain photographs ever taken in Colorado. His tradition, born from the work by the great W. H. Jackson, is carried on by mountain enthusiasts who strive to achieve the quality of photographic art which Standley attained. Photo from authors' collection

A 1925 photograph shows a visitor rounding the Grand View Overlook at the Bottomless Pit on the Pikes Peak Highway. The precipice is one of the spectacular stops along the route with a drop of more than 1,700 vertical feet. It was carved by glacial action during the Ice Ages. Photo from authors' collection

The April snowdrifts on the tracks of the Pikes Peak Cog Railroad were removed by a flatcar snowplow which was slipped under the snow at track level, then raised sideways, dumping the snow on the downhill side. In this 1925 photograph you can see the solid snow wall on the right and the stacks of deposited snow on the left. Photo from authors' collection

This view shows Colorado Springs as it looked after the Depression began in 1930, from the summit of Pikes Peak. A full moon lights up the usually dark back side of Camerons Cone and Mount Manitou Park. The population in 1930 was 33,237. Photo courtesy of Jim Bates

The Cog Wheel route of the Manitou and Pikes Peak Railway is one of the highest cog railroads in the world. Here a 1930 engine pushes a passenger car up the twenty-five percent grade of Big Hill. Almagre Mountain is in the background. Photo from authors' collection

In 1929 Clarence Coil, Doug Shafer, and John Fowler of the Colorado Mountain Club organized the Silver Spruce Ski Club and built a run north from Woodland Park near Edlowe, on the Silver Spruce Ranch. The hill and a cabin at the base were leased to them for ten dollars a month by Mr. and Mrs. E. J. Merriman, owners of the ranch. Here a jumper tests the chilly air above Suicide Hill. Photo courtesy of Pioneers' Museum

In the late 1930s, the Silver Spruce Ski Club moved its activities up onto Pikes Peak below Glen Cove, where the first rope tow west of the Mississippi was built. Don Lawrie, one of the original members of the club, demonstrates the parallel turn on wood skis at Pikes Peak. The lack of metal edges made controlled carved turns rather difficult. Photo courtesy of Pioneers' Museum

C. B. Keller landed this aeroplane at the McLaughlin Lodge airfield in Manitou, on 8 May 1928. McLaughlin's was the only campground and cottage city in the United States that had its own airport. Photo from authors' collection

LINDBERGH'S ENDORSEMENT

CHAS. A. LINDBERGH
Trans-Atlantic Flyer

St. Louis, Mo.,
February 24, 1927.

Alexander Aircraft Co.,
Denver, Colorado.

Gentlemen:

I wish to add my small share to the general sentiment for your Eaglerock. I have been rather skeptical on the average "New Production" job for "commercial" work.

At the present moment my opinion is entirely changed. I never hoped to see any OX-5 motored ship perform as the Eaglerock performed for me during the severe test I gave it some days ago. I have never felt as though I could trust implicitly in any new production commercial ship, until I had the pleasure of piloting this Eaglerock. I climbed in doubtful and climbed out a convert.

It is the most beautifully performing thing I have ever flown. It has strength and a degree of maneuverability heretofore considered hopeless in any aircraft.

I am, of course, speaking of commercial ships and not of army pursuit or other high-powered army types.

Very truly yours,
CHARLES A. LINDBERGH,
Chief Pilot, St. Louis-Chicago Air Mail.

🍀 🍀 🍀

SLIM'S CHOICE

In February, 1927, Slim Lindbergh flew an OX-5 motored Eaglerock and his enthusiasm over its performance led him to ask the demonstrators from the Alexander Aircraft Company to build him a Whirlwind motored job for the New York to Paris hop.

President J. Don Alexander realized the importance of Lindbergh's offer and agreed with him that a Whirlwind motored Eaglerock was a logical job for the trip but—orders for the standard type Eaglerock needed to be filled and rather than break the line of production, Lindbergh's offer was rejected.

Let all due credit be given to the intrepid and successful flyer, his gallant ship and the Whirlwind motor that carried through. The fact still remains, that the—

EAGLEROCK WAS SLIM'S CHOICE

This endorsement by a famous aviator adequately describes the Alexander Eaglerock Airplaine of 1927. Photos courtesy of Pioneers' Museum

157

In 1930 J. Don Alexander, president of Alexander Industries, offered the Boy Scout Glider Troop the use of Alexander Aircraft Company facilities, where they built their own glider, patterned after one of Alexander's models.

Shown in this picture are: Howard Dostal, F. H. Engstrom, Wade McKinley, Lester Peck, Joe Kamionka, Charles Page, John Innes, Bill Shanks, Ray Ebeling, Howard Pick, John Todd, Donald Newton and John Adams. Photo courtesy of John Innes

The Blind Pedestrian's Appeal
To the motorist behind the wheel:

WHEN you see my cane and pilot white,
Remember all with me is dark as night.
I cannot see your path or speed,
And, therefore, I can take no heed.
I will follow my pilot true,
And then leave all the rest to you,
If there should an accident be,
Death and not the blame would fall on me.
Death rides the highway all the time
Remember it's left for me to do?

I know your heart is always right
Toward those of us who have no sight.
Help us, then, to give a pilot white
To your dear friend who has no sight.
We are trying to work out our salvation
In this modern world of motorization.
Uncle Peter's White Cane and Pilot White
Saves His long life by day or night.

Colorado Springs — The Birthplace of the White Cane Idea in America and the Home of the White Pilot Club.

Colorado Springs was the birthplace of the white cane idea for the blind and the home of the White Pilot Club, organized in 1928. Photo from authors' collection

The Marjorie Palmer Watt Nutrition Camp was the chief project of the Junior League in 1931.

The camp was founded in 1923 through the interest and generosity of Mrs. Henry C. Watt and was managed by a board of eleven directors. By arrangement with Beth-El Hospital, whose buildings were used, one dollar a day covered the cost per child. Pictured are nurses from Beth-El with some of the younger children. Photo from authors' collection

The Sinton Dairy Company was established in 1880 by George H. and Melvin M. Sinton. In 1887 they built a new dairy plant in the 400 block on South El Paso Street. They visited the elementary schools of the region, demonstrated the milking method and served the warm bubbly milk to the children. Photo from authors' collection

Students of Helen Hunt School are ready to experience milk fresh from the cow. Photo from authors' collection

The Salvation Army food program started in Colorado Springs about 1889 when the Army was organized here. This photo was taken at Christmastime 1930, at the City Auditorium where food was distributed to the needy. The food program is still carried on by the Salvation Army during the Christmas season. Photo courtesy of Penrose Public Library

159

During the Franklin D. Roosevelt administration a Works Progress Association camp was set up in the southeast corner of Palmer Park. Two hundred men constructed roads, trails, and picnic area improvements. Occupants of the neighboring Civilian Conservation Corps camp improved the Templeton Gap flood control. Photo from authors' collection

This photo of Monument Valley Park before the 1935 flood shows the bath house, swimming pool, and one of the formal English gardens. The park was a gift to the city from General William Jackson Palmer in 1907, and the pool was added by Spencer and Julie Penrose in 1914. Photo courtesy of Pioneers' Museum

These two photographs show the outstanding botanical collection in the rock garden of Monument Valley Park. This was built with a strong English influence, and, indeed, these gardens might suggest Kew. They were destroyed by the 1935 Memorial Day flood, and the site has been nothing like it since. Photo courtesy of Pioneers' Museum

This photo of the Broadmoor as it looked in 1935 shows the hotel (center), the golf club (lower center), Penrose Stadium (left), Pauline Chapel (upper left), and Cheyenne School (upper right). Photo courtesy of Pioneers' Museum

Every stream in the Pikes Peak region overflowed during the Memorial Day flood of 1935. Several people were killed and property damage amounted to millions of dollars. This is Cheyenne Road near the old Stratton Park, under the floodwaters of Cheyenne Creek. Photo courtesy of Penrose Public Library

COLD SPRINGS

The Memorial Day flood of 1935 was the most destructive flood ever recorded in Pikes Peak country. Here, Monument Creek destroys the gardens of Monument Valley Park. Photo courtesy of Pioneers' Museum

Two of the people who drowned during the 1935 Memorial Day flood can be seen standing on the roof of a car in this photo, taken on Nevada Avenue. Their bodies were never recovered. Photo courtesy of Pioneers' Museum

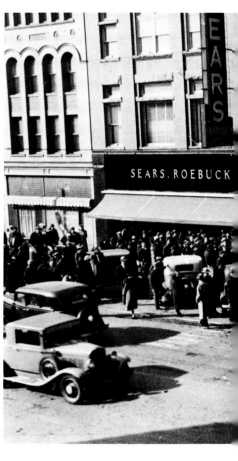

FINE ARTS CENTER
1936

The Colorado Springs Fine Arts Center began in October 1919 when Mr. and Mrs. Spencer Penrose offered their home on 30 West Dale to the Art Society for an art center. With an annual endowment of $1,000 the society accepted and the board of trustees appointed officers: Mrs. Penrose, president; Mr. D. V. Donaldson, vice-president; and Mrs. Anne Ritter; Mr. F. D. Smith; and Mrs. C. L. Tutt as members. With the merger completed the center was named the Broadmoor Art Academy. In 1931 Mrs. Meredith Hare and Mrs. Alice Bemis Taylor successfully proposed a new larger building at the site to house an extensive collection of regional art, and Mrs. Penrose approved. On 4 January 1935 the name was changed to the Colorado Springs Fine Arts Center. The multi-purpose concrete building, designed by John Gaw Meem, was completed in April 1936. The museum now houses an extensive collection of western and Indian art including works by Bierstadt, Inness, and Moran. A theater hosts musical and theatrical productions, and a recital room is frequented by music students and concert artists who perform everything from Cage to Chopin. Photo from the authors' collection

The Venetucci family took over the Haigler Ranch south of Colorado Springs in May 1936 during the Depression when alfalfa sold for six dollars a ton and hogs for five dollars per hundred weight. The success of the ranch was assured when, after experimentation with fifty varieties of corn, the famous Venetucci golden bantam sweet corn was developed.

In addition to corn, the Venetucci brothers, Tony and Nick, grow pumpkins, and each year before Halloween they invite all the townschildren to come pick a pumpkin. Photo from authors' collection

On 23 February 1939 the J. C. Penney Company held a fire sale to clear out stock damaged by the fire a few days earlier. Here a mob of bargain hunters wait for the doors to open. Photo courtesy of Penrose Public Library

Among the fringed surrey hack drivers was Ma (Nora) Gaines. She could out-swear, out-fight, and out-wit any driver for a fare. This picture shows her at the back of her hack parked across the street from the Y.M.C.A. Photo from authors' collection

The entire town turned out for the Santa Claus Parade sponsored by the Merchants   *Association during the Christmas season of 1939. Photo courtesy of Penrose Library*

World War II
and the
New Industry

10 CHAPTER
1941~1954

World War II began a new era for the city of Colorado Springs, a scenario not yet completed. Efforts to obtain a military base were successful, and in 1941-42, Camp Carson was established south of the city. Visions of new industry and economic growth were on the minds of the city fathers at that time. Tourism had been the principle industry, and a seasonal one at that. World War II cut travel down dramatically with gas rationing, and many local hotels used real horsepower to cart their guests around to the regional attractions. Many old automobiles were converted from tank-dry uselessness to horse-drawn carriages. After the war, when stability and economic growth returned, the military camp grew and so did Colorado Springs. Men who were stationed here during the war returned to retire, a tradition which continues to this day. The population of Colorado Springs grew from 36,000 to 50,000 during the period. In 1954, Camp Carson became a full-fledged fort. However this was only the beginning of the military impact upon Colorado Springs.

During the World War II years, tourism remained an important business in Colorado Springs. Transportation companies such as the Pikes Peak Stage Lines outfitted coaches like these to carry tourists to the area attractions. These Cuneo coaches cost the line more than $6,000. Photo courtesy of Pioneers' Museum

With gasoline in short supply during World War II, horse teams were harnessed to converted automobiles, to carry tourists from their hotels to the sights of the region.

The Great Western Stage, shown here, ran from the Antlers Hotel to Manitou. Photo courtesy of Pioneers' Museum

169

This is how the Colorado Springs Airport looked in 1941, before the army moved in and took over. On 6 January 1942 Colorado Springs was chosen to host Camp Carson, a decision which completely changed the history and role of the city. Photo courtesy of Pioneers' Museum

The corps of military police from Camp Carson worked with the city of Colorado Springs in law enforcement after the army post was established. In the center of this 1945 photograph is I. B. "Dad" Bruce, then chief of police for the city. Photo from authors' collection

The Pikes Peak or Bust Rodeo has been an annual tradition in Colorado Springs since 1936, except for the war years. Pre-rodeo events are held to spark interest and enthusiasm for the show.

This is one of the first street breakfasts, held in downtown Colorado Springs on 1 August 1946. The author and her father are in this photo. Photo courtesy of Pioneers' Museum

my Good Friend.
dad Bruce.
my Very Best Wishes.
Leo J Cremer
Rodeo 51

*Leo J. Cremer was one of the early
promoters of the Pikes Peak or Bust Rodeo
after World War II. Photo from authors'
collection*

*Max Morath advocated ragtime and one-
man shows before either became popular.*

*A native of Colorado Springs and 1948
graduate of Colorado College, Max studied
piano and formal composition and learned
to play "ragtime style" from his mother,
Mrs. Gladys Morath.*

*Max Morath is truly an American
performer committed to a purely American
art form. Photo courtesy of* Gazette-
Telegraph

Harry "Chico" Galbraith and Colonel Ingmire watch the packing of one of the mules in preparation for the ascent of Barr Trail on Pikes Peak. The mules, which came from Camp Carson, packed gear up to the summit for the Flag Day celebration on June 1949. Photo from authors' collection

Heavily packed mules and soldiers from Camp Carson begin the arduous thirteen-mile climb of Pikes Peak from Manitou, via the Barr Trail for the Flag Day ceremony at the summit in June 1949.

The trail was laid out from 1914 to 1918 by Fred Barr, a charter member of the Ad-Am-An Club of Colorado Springs, formed in 1923 for the purpose of giving a pyrotechnic fireworks display from Pikes Peak each New Year's Eve. Photo from authors' collection

Above 13,000 feet elevation on Barr Trail one of the pack mules loses its footing and "goes down." These switchbacks across the east face of the peak and the thirteen golden stairs section are rough and boulder-strewn, making footing unsure and tough. Photo from authors' collection

General Gill from Camp Carson speaks to a crowd on Flag Day 1949 at the summit of Pikes Peak. On General Gill's right is Rene Gagnon of Iwo Jima fame; to his left are an unidentified member of the Ad-Am-An Club, Harry Standley, Don Lawrie, and Willis Magee. Gagnon commented that although the altitude was a bit tough, this flag-raising was easier than the one on Iwo Jima. Photo from authors' collection

Soldiers from Camp Carson haul equipment up the Barr Trail to the summit of Pikes Peak for the 1949 flag-raising ceremony. Before the peak was scaled by roads, supplies were hauled in this manner to the United States Army Signal Station on the summit. Here, at over 13,000 feet altitude, simple walking is tough work. Photo courtesy of Pioneers' Museum

The American flag was raised on the 14,110 foot high summit of Pikes Peak on 14 June 1949. Photo from authors' collection

The cannon salute from the summit of Pikes Peak was given by soldiers from Camp Carson on 14 June 1949. Photo from authors' collection

The modern Pikes Peak Hill Climb has been taking place every July 4, and it draws large crowds of people who sometimes camp on the mountain in order to have a good watchspot for the race. No drivers have had more impact upon the race than the local Uncer family. Louie Uncer dominated the race after World War II and the tradition was passed down in their family to Al and Bobby Uncer, who broke their own records year after year on the mountain during the 1960s. Today, Bobby Uncer, Jr. has appeared as another Pikes Peak Hill Climb force to be reckoned with. Photo from authors' collection

The Newton Lumber Company Float is inspected before the 1952 Pikes Peak or Bust Rodeo parade. The parade is one of several annual events connected with preceding the rodeo. Photo from authors' collection

The Half Century Club met at the home of Mrs. Harry Jones in 1951. Then, as now, few people had spent fifty or more years in the Pikes Peak region. From left to right are: seated, Mrs. F. T. Sanders, Elizabeth Laura Douglass, Mrs. Kittie Fryhofer, Mrs. Emma Douglass Nicholson, Mrs. Emma Young; standing, Mr. Edward Brown, Mr. L. T. Spielman, Mrs. Helen Akin, Kirke Douglass, and Mrs. Frances Spielman Ricken. Photo from authors' collection

Collecting rock specimens is a common hobby in this region of superlative geology. Mr. and Mrs. W. E. Crosby were collectors of petrified wood, and at their Ruxton Avenue home they assembled over a ton of specimens. Photo courtesy of Pioneers' Museum

A 1952 aerial view of Peterson Field. This was the old City of Colorado Springs Airport, established in 1925. In 1926 Robert Rhea influenced the city to buy 640 additional acres, and in June 1942 there was an unsuccessful attempt to rename the airport for him. The city divided its interest in the airport with the army in 1941, and on 13 December 1942 it was officially named Peterson Field for Lieutenant Edward J. Peterson. Photo courtesy of Pioneers' Museum

In 1954 Camp Carson was upgraded and reclassified as Fort Carson. Permanent buildings were erected, and the land area was gradually expanded. Fort Carson today is a multi-faceted military installation, reflective of the new concepts of the Modern Volunteer Army. Photo from authors' collection

Samuel Hoy Brown V, son of Dr. and Mrs. Samuel H. Brown, presents an 1812 American Flag to Lieutenant Colonel George Bennett at Fort Carson in 1956. Samuel is now a Lieutenant Colonel stationed at Ramstein Air Force Base, Germany. Photo courtesy of Pioneers' Museum

One of the most beloved teachers in Colorado Springs was Dr. Lloyd Shaw of Cheyenne Mountain Schools. Dr. Shaw was once served a plate of cooked earthworms by his biology class; earlier he had told this class in a lecture that earthworms were edible.

His love was the square dance, and his students won many awards during the 1950s. These were some of his "high swingers" at the school amphitheater, behind the present Canon Elementary School. Photo courtesy of Pioneers' Museum

During the 1950s, when baseball was the American game, the Sky Sox of Colorado Springs represented the city in semi-professional baseball competition. Photo courtesy of Penrose Public Library

The Historical Society of the Pikes Peak region has always been active in identifying and preserving places of historic value in this area. In June 1955 they dedicated the house where "Queen" Palmer taught school, the first public school in Colorado Springs (1871). Standing is Raymond Caldwell and Dorothy Weinburger, with Gene Weinburger kneeling. Photo from authors' collection

Welcome Home! Another win by the successful Colorado Springs Sky Sox at Memorial Park. The Sox played against semi-professional baseball teams from all across the midwestern United States during the 1950s. Photo courtesy of Penrose Public Library

An Amarillo player slides safely home during an August 1952 baseball game at Memorial Park in Colorado Springs. However the Sky Sox won this contest 4 2. Photo courtesy of Penrose Public Library

This was youth sign-up day in 1956 for one of the baseball camps offered by the Colorado Springs Sky Sox. Photo courtesy of Penrose Public Library

A moment of excitement during a June 1959 baseball game between teams sponsored by Ent Air Force Base and Shook's Grocery. The tradition of business-sponsored baseball has not vanished from Colorado Springs, and Memorial Field is often the setting for a fun filled evening during the summer.

Ent Air Force Base is now the site of the United States Olympic Committee and Training Center. Photo courtesy of Penrose Public Library

Whether or not the Sky Sox won, they were winners and warmly supported by the fans in Colorado Springs as seen in this 1956 parade on Tejon Street. Photo courtesy of Penrose Public Library

Colorado
Springs into
the Space Age

11 CHAPTER 1955~1969

Colorado Springs launched into national recognition again during this period. The Air Force announced that its official collegiate training institution would locate here, and the United States Air Force Academy became the most popular attraction in Colorado. When Sputnik was launched, it shocked Americans into a new awareness of science. The ability to track missiles and space objects became a priority of national defense, and the North American Air Defense Command built its nerve center in the hard granite batholith of Cheyenne Mountain during the early sixties. In 1969 the Broadmoor World Arena hosted another World Figure Skating Championship, and Gabriele Seyfert took the place of the beloved Peggy Fleming. This event foreshadowed the national significance of sports in Colorado Springs. The economy, business, and stability of the city was solidly assured. From 1955 to 1969 the population of Colorado Springs grew from 50,000 to 130,000 people. The Colorado Springs native was becoming a rare, almost endangered species. The trend has continued relentlessly.

During the 1950s Colorado Springs was the short-length movie capital of the world. The Alexander Film Company was then the world's largest producer-distributor of short-length theater screen advertising. The company began in Spokane, Washington in 1919 and moved to Denver in 1924 where aircraft manufacture began. In 1928 the entire operation moved to Colorado Springs. The company was built by its founders, J. Don and Don M. Alexander. Photo from authors' collection

The Alexander Film Company served more than 21,000 advertisers across the United States during the 1950s. More than half of the 17,000 theaters in the nation at that time displayed Alexander service, as well as some 1,500 theaters in twelve foreign countries. The monthly studio production averaged 3,640,000 feet of film. Photo from authors' collection

This was a typical film shooting scene at the Alexander Film Company studios. After a minute or so, the director would signal the cut and another advertising short would be under production. The models would shed their jewels and fur coats and return to their more prosaic secretarial and stenographic jobs. Photo from authors' collection

On 22 June 1954 Secretary of the Air Force Harold E. Talbott announced the selection of the permanent site of the United States Air Force Academy, seven miles north of Colorado Springs. Seventeen thousand five hundred acres of land were acquired and construction began. On 2 September 1958 the first classes started at the $200 million campus. Photo from authors' collection

The all-faith Air Force Academy Chapel is the most striking building on the academy campus. Scaled by Walter Netsch and built by Skidmore, Owings and Merrill to fit the Space Age, its seventeen soaring spires cost $3.5 million. Photo courtesy of Penrose Public Library

A lesson is given at the organ amid the breathtaking color of the inspiring Air Force Academy Chapel. Photo from authors' collection

*Frank Lloyd Wright came to Colorado
Springs to see the Air Force Academy Chapel
during its construction. This sequence shows
the assembly of what is one of the most
unusual buildings in the world. Photo
courtesy of Penrose Public Library*

190

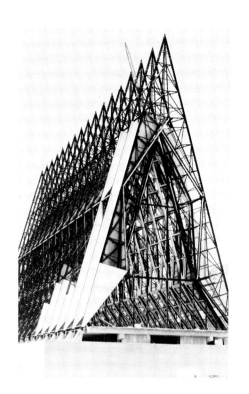

The Air Force Academy teaches some 3,200 cadets many disciplines from astronautics to vertebrate embryology. In the Air Force Academy Planetarium, cadets learn about astronomy and charting the stars, and at certain times during the year, well-planned, educational, and entertaining shows are given to the public. Photo from authors' collection

President John F. Kennedy visited Colorado Springs on 5 June 1963 when he addressed the graduating class of the United States Air Force Academy. Crowds of people lined the streets, hoping to get a glimpse of the president going to and from the academy. Photo courtesy of Pioneers' Museum

During the early 1960s the hard granite of Cheyenne Mountain was hollowed out to make room for the North American Air Defense Command (NORAD) complex. This center is responsible for giving the first warning of an aerial attack against North America. Photo courtesy of United States Air Force

A 4,675-foot long tunnel connects the north and south portals with the interior entrance to the NORAD complex. The interior entrance is shielded by huge steel blast doors which would glancingly deflect a nuclear blast on through to the other end of the tunnel. Photo courtesy of United States Air Force

This is one of the massive steel blast doors, 1,200 feet inside the access tunnel to NORAD. Each door is more than three feet thick and weighs twenty-five tons. A hydrolic mechanism can open or close each door in thirty seconds. Photo courtesy of United States Air Force

Photographs show two of the eleven, three-story buildings in the NORAD cavern, one finished and the other under construction. The free-standing structures are made from ⅜-inch continuous weld steel plates and provide over 200,000 square feet of floor space. Photo courtesy of United States Air Force

The buildings of the NORAD complex are supported upon massive steel springs, designed to protect the sensitive electronic equipment. The 1,319 springs are made from three-inch-diameter steel and each weighs a half ton. Shock absorbers help minimize bounce and sway in case of an outside nuclear explosion. Photo courtesy of United States Air Force

Defense information may originate at the Distant Early Warning (DEW) Line in Greenland or a Ballistic Missile Early Warning System in Alaska and pass through the computer onto the display screens without ever being processed by human hands. Photo courtesy of United States Air Force

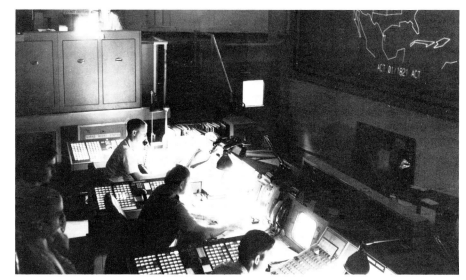

The command post of NORAD features two 12-foot-by-16-foot display screens which form the forward wall. The display technician can construct a scene of North America which shows the paths of unidentified aircraft approaching the continent. Photo courtesy of United States Air Force

Helen Hunt Falls, a forty-foot drop in North Cheyenne Canyon Park, was named for the famous author who lived and wrote in this region. In March 1966 the city of Colorado Springs Park and Recreation Department placed this marker at the falls. Standing are: C. W. "Red" Luce (left), and W. M. Bartlett (right). Seated are: Harold Seeley of the El Paso County Pioneers' Association (left), and Helen Jackson, great niece of Helen Hunt Jackson (right). Photo from authors' collection

In February 1962 the sister city relationship between Colorado Springs and Fuji-Yoshida, Japan was commemorated with this monument and garden on Nevada Avenue next to Acacia Park. Photo from authors' collection

Fountain Creek is shown destroying a bridge during the August 1965 flood. Photo courtesy of Pioneers' Museum

This house on Cheyenne Creek below Mayhurst nearly became a houseboat during the flood of 1965. Many bridges washed away, isolating the Broadmoor from Colorado Springs. Photo courtesy of Pioneers' Museum

Soldiers from Fort Carson are shown sandbagging along Cheyenne Creek during the powerful August 1965 flood.

Fortunately, there were very few injuries considering the magnitude of the flood. Photo courtesy of Pioneers' Museum

In May 1967 the National Park Service of the United States Department of the Interior announced a master plan for the Colorado Petrified Forest area to be included in Florissant Fossil Beds National Monument. Soon afterward the plan became reality and the Pikes Peak region acquired its first national park.

This is a fossil stump of Sequoioxylon pearsallii, seventy-four feet in circumference and fifteen feet high. Sequoia stumps were popular attractions at numerous world's fairs and exhibitions before 1900, and many great trees were destroyed including at least four larger than the reigning champion, General Sherman, in California. When the stumps at Florissant were discovered, they too were vandalized; this stump was to be removed in sections and reassembled at the 1893 Chicago World's Fair for exhibit. However, the agate was harder than the sawblades, which broke and were permanently imbedded in the stone. Photo courtesy of Pioneers' Museum

Colorado College is a private liberal arts college which combines the instructional quality of the Ivy League schools with the dynamic environment of Colorado Springs and the Pikes Peak region. General William Jackson Palmer set aside six blocks for the future site of a college in 1871. The Reverend T. N. Haskell from the

University of Wisconsin suggested a Christian college be started in Colorado in 1872, and on 4 January 1874 the decision was unanimously carried. Classes began on 6 May 1874 under the guidance of Colorado College's first president, Reverend Jonathan Edwards. The college consistently hires top professional instructors, such as

Hanya Holm, choreographer of Kiss Me Kate and My Fair Lady, Reah Sadowsky, concert pianist and student on the legendary Josef Lhevinne, and Richard Pearl, the geologists' geologist and author of the books on Rocky Mountain minerals. Photo from authors' collection

Contemporary
Colorado
Springs

12 CHAPTER 1970 ~ 1981

Modern Colorado Springs is a many faceted gem. To pinpoint a single direction of growth or change pertaining to the city is hardly possible. As the city turns toward new fields of development, like the revolving gem, new facets appear and old ones capture new light in previously unseen ways.

While Colorado Springs has bright sides and some brilliant ones, it also has its dark sides. With its unprecedented growth has come increased crime, and hardly anyone remains untouched by it. Traffic snarls, once unknown, are now as frustrating here as in any large city. The solitude of the mountain parks is just a memory in the minds of those who have lived here for any considerable length of time.

Yet, 'The Springs' retains much of the special character of its past, enough to attract thousands of new residents and millions of tourists each year. This character is a Renaissance atmosphere in the setting of some of the most spectacular scenery on the North American continent. Art, business, culture, history, music, science, sports, and theater are alive and well in Colorado Springs. They interact with each other in a wonderful way, and bring to our people a more universal understanding of harmony.

Einstein said that the only universal constant is change. This is the only certainty of the future of Colorado Springs. It will grow and it will change again. Upon the brows of those people who plan for the future lies the enormous responsibility of maintaining as much positive character of this city as possible. And upon the new citizen lies the responsibility of learning about Colorado Springs—so that the special uniqueness of this city will not deteriorate into memory. The natives and longtime residents bear the role of mentors to teach the absolute truths and strive to preserve the ultimate human values which are the life-blood of Colorado Springs. With some fears, some memories, some ideas, and some plans, we anticipate the future.

The city of Colorado Springs is seen from the summit of Pikes Peak, elevation 14,110 feet, during the Ad-Am-An climb and fireworks display on New Year's Eve, 1980. While the view east from the summit of the mountain can extend beyond the Kansas border, the city itself only covers a bit more than 100 square miles of the area—about two-thirds of the lighted area shown. The original layout of the city by General Palmer can be seen as the dense, bright cluster of lights just right from the center of the photograph and left of the black shadow of Camerons Cone and Mount Arthur. Photo courtesy of Jim Bates

Since 1970 urban renewal struck parts of downtown Colorado Springs, razing blocks of old buildings. Government buildings and parking lots replaced them, and a few notable old buildings were saved and renovated. This photo looks west from the Pioneers' Museum, toward the new El Paso County Courthouse (left), Centennial Hall (center), and the El Paso County Jail (right). The new theater-auditorium can be seen under construction. It will be the new performing home for the Colorado Springs Symphony. Photo from authors' collection

Spoon Falls, also called Silver Cascade Falls, is a Tahitian-like film of water which drops in sheets over a smooth granite skin in Buffalo Canyon, near Helen Hunt Falls. The 150-foot high drop is named for the circular scallop in the granite where falling water is forced vertically into the air like a geyser. This photo shows a thirty-foot tall fountain ricocheting from the spoon. The granite is slick and the lure of the falls is tempting; through the years over a dozen people have slipped and fallen to their deaths here. The falls were very popular when Bruin Inn was in its heyday before 1950. Photo from authors' collection

Fort Carson, south of Colorado Springs, continues to have a large impact upon the city of Colorado Springs and other communities of the Pikes Peak region. The army is a very controversial subject in Colorado Springs where military and civilian activities are often joint ventures. Photo from authors' collection

The barracks on Fort Carson are modern units, very similar to college dormitories and house single, enlisted personnel. With the addition of chapels, a commissary, a gymnasium, a hospital, family housing, and other comforts, the army post is becoming a modern, self-contained unit with attractive benefits in behalf of its people. Many distinguished people who were stationed at Fort Carson in the past, return to Colorado Springs to live during their retirement. Photo from authors' collection

The progressive programs and abundant opportunities at Fort Carson make the post very attractive to officers, recruits, and enlisted personnel. The army is quickly removing the "Brown Shoe" image as it advances into the Space Age. Photo from authors' collection

A 1976 photo shows Peterson Air Force Base in the upper right and the Colorado Springs Municipal Airport in the lower left. Peterson Field was reclassified and upgraded to an official Air Force Base in 1976, shortly before this photo was taken. Photo courtesy of Pioneers' Museum

The High Flight Foundation is an American spiritual organization located in Colorado Springs and is dedicated to spiritual awareness and the religious heritage of Americans and their relationship with God. Colonel James B. Irwin, explorer of the moon during Apollo XV, became aware of his relationship with God during the historic moon walk. Inspired by his encounter, the charismatic Irwin founded High Flight and has been highly active in teaching people about Christ ever since. Photo courtesy of James B. Irwin and High Flight

The impact of Space Age industry upon Colorado Springs has been enormous since 1970. While national manufacturing growth increased by 75 percent during this period, in Colorado Springs it mushroomed by a staggering 170 percent. Aerospace products, aircraft instruments, computers, electronics, solar energy, and other industries have settled here, many of national importance. This is an assembly of these businesses in the Pikes Peak Industrial Park. Photo from authors' collection

From June to August 1978 Colorado Springs was bombarded by no fewer than five major hailstorms which caused millions of dollars worth of property damage. Softball-sized ice chunks fell to depths of several feet in some places. Here, a wall of melting hail descended upon the Broadmoor West Hotel, doing great damage. Many trees were stressed into reflowering or putting on new, abnormal growth. A ponderosa pine, felled in the Broadmoor area in 1980, showed two thin but distinctly separate growth rings for the year 1978, the only such record in the 278 year history of that tree. Photo courtesy of Gazette Telegraph

During the summer of 1979 Colorado Springs experienced a series of great rarities—tornados. After touching down several times in Manitou and West Colorado Springs, the funnel seen in the upper left hand corner of this photo hovered and drifted over the downtown of Colorado Springs. Tornadoes form in the mountains but do not remain on the ground for more than a few seconds if they actually touch down at all. Photo courtesy of Gazette Telegraph

The statue of The Man on the Iron Horse, at the intersection of Platte and Nevada is shown from Acacia Park. The man is General William Jackson Palmer, founder of Colorado Springs in 1871. The auditorium of Palmer High School looms in the background. Photo from authors' collection

This house in West Colorado Springs was destroyed during the tornado of June 1978. The author witnessed the storm and its destruction here and now seeks shelter when a tornado warning is issued. Photo courtesy of Gazette Telegraph

English architecture dominated Colorado Springs after General Palmer founded the city. The Grace Church was built by W. S. Stratton in 1873 and is among several fine local buildings of English Gothic style. Now known as the Village Inn, it is a fine restaurant. It was the meeting place of the Pikes Peak Posse of the Westerners, *a society dedicated to historic preservation of the west. Photo from authors' collection*

The American Red Cross, organized in 1881, is celebrating its centennial. This is their headquarters in Colorado Springs at 1600 North Cascade Avenue. The Pikes Peak chapter is very active in first aid instruction and information. The United Way also headquarters here, as well as the business office of the Colorado Springs Symphony, upstairs. Photo from authors' collection

Dr. Richard Beidleman and Helen Jackson exchange ideas on a hot summer afternoon at Colorado College. Helen Jackson, great niece of Helen Hunt Jackson, devotes her time to teaching, speaking, and being a delightful person. She is often at the Pioneers' Museum where the Jackson house is displayed. Dr. Beidleman is the John Muir of the Pikes Peak region. A professor at Colorado College, he is a biologist ecologist-naturalist who refuses to release his popsicle wrapper except into the confines of a trash can. Photo from authors' collection

The Broadmoor World Arena, part of the expansive Broadmoor complex, has been the site of numerous regional, national, and world figure skating competitions. Many national and world champions such as David and Hayes Jenkins, Peggy Fleming, and Tim Wood trained here. The World Arena also hosts Western Hockey League games between Colorado College and opponents from across the nation, plus the international Walter Brown Cup, a hockey tournament hosting teams from Canada, Czechoslovakia, the Soviet Union, and the United States. There is also a curling rink and tournaments of this little-known sport are held here.

The United States Figure Skating Association National Headquarters and Hall of Fame moved to Colorado Springs in 1979. Located near the famous World Arena, the museum preserves the bright history and impact which American figure skating has had upon the world. Photo from authors' collection

In 1979 Colorado Springs earned another landmark of national interest when the Prorodeo Hall of Champions and Museum of the American Cowboy located here. The PRCA national headquarters features artwork by and about cowboys, including such famous artists as Remington, Russel, Scriver, and Phippen. Photo from authors' collection

With an average of 300 days of sunshine per year, it is only natural that Colorado Springs would be attractive to solar energy research and development. A massive parabolic solar collector system may be seen on the roof of this local motor inn. Active and passive systems are expensive, but with constant refinement their efficiency soon pays for the expense. Depending on the type and capacity of the collector, a reduction of energy cost from thirty percent to more than ninety percent can be attained. This collector, developed by local research, is eleven times more efficient than the more common flat 1:1 solar collector. Photo from authors' collection

This is the entrance to the United States Olympic Training Center, where athletes from across the nation train in hope of representing the United States in Olympic and World competition.

The flags are the banners of various national sports federations whose athletes train at this center. Photo from authors' collection

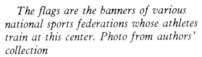

The first National Sports Festival was held in Colorado Springs in 1978. The USOC decision to headquarter here and the impact of the National Sports Festival may be the most significant events in the modern history of Colorado Springs. Photo from authors' collection

The headquarters for the United States Olympic Committee is in this building, the Olympic House in Colorado Springs. Photo from authors' collection

This photo shows the United States National Sports Building on the campus of the Olympic Training Center, Colorado Springs. Photo from authors' collection

A group of young athletes walk past the Helsinki building on their way to the track and field area, on the campus of the USOC Training Center. Photo from authors' collection

Two unidentified boxers test their strength, stamina, and spirit during the 1978 National Sports Festival, Colorado Springs, Colorado. Photo courtesy of United States Olympic Committee Archives

Tracee Talavera performs in the balance beam event of the gymnastics competition at the 1979 National Sports Festival, Colorado Springs, Colorado. Photo courtesy of United States Olympic Committee Archives

Al Oerter displays his awesome gold medal talent in the discus event at the 1979 National Sports Festival. Photo courtesy of United States Olympic Committee Archives

· *And they're off! The gun cracks to the thunder of 800 runners who dared the world's toughest footrace—The Pikes Peak Marathon. The runners will climb 7,500 vertical feet along the thirteen mile Barr Trail to the 14,110 foot summit of Pikes Peak, then return to the finish line at Ruxton and Manitou Avenue. The race involves 15,000 feet of altitude and twenty-six miles of winding, sometimes boulder-strewn trail. One exhausted marathoner, veteran of many such races across the country said, "The Boston Marathon is a pea-shooter, a mild, Sunday stroll compared to this."*

Pat Porter of Adams State College set a new record during the ascent run, 8 August 1981. His time was shattered during the roundtrip race the next day when Al Waquie of Jemez Pueblo, New Mexico ran it in a blistering 2:05:47, seven minutes faster than Porter. Photo from authors' collection

Al Waquie, an Indian from Jemez Pueblo, New Mexico, crosses the finish line fresh as a flower, and wins the 1981 Pikes Peak Marathon. His incredible pace was two hours faster than each of the first five cars to drive to the summit of Pikes Peak. Photo from authors' collection

Photographers and news media celebrities gather to interview Al Waquie who finished this toughest marathon in record time—3:26:17, more than five minutes better than the old record and twenty minutes ahead of his nearest rival. His cousin, Steven Gachupin, won the race six straight times from 1966 to 1971. The race was first organized by Rudy Fahl more than thirty years ago. Photo from authors' collection

The Bicentennial of the United States and the Centennial of Colorado were celebrated in Memorial Park by a crowd of 80,000 people. Here is the vast fireworks display immediately following the Tchaikovsky 1812 Festival Overture, played in a bravissimo *performance by the Colorado Springs Symphony, Colorado Springs Chorale, and cannons from Fort Carson, under the direction of Maestro Charles Ansbacher. The smoke from the cannon can be seen drifting below the fireworks. Photo courtesy of* Gazette Telegraph

Conductor Charles Ansbacher leads the Colorado Springs Symphony Orchestra through The Planets, *by Gustav Holst, to the delight of thousands. Each summer the orchestra performs a half-dozen or more free concerts in the city parks, culminating with the Fourth of July celebration in Memorial Park.*

213

A gathering of people assemble on the lawn of the Pioneers' Museum, formerly the El Paso County Courthouse, to listen to a summer symphony program given by the Colorado Springs Symphony. Photo courtesy of Gazette Telegraph

If you were the timpanist of the Colorado Springs Symphony Orchestra, you would often have this view. Here, the conductor cues the bass drum during a tense moment of Rossini's William Tell Overture, *at a summer symphony concert. Photo from authors' collection*

During the later summer after the crops are ready for harvest, the Farmers Market, sponsored by the Colorado State University Extension Service is held in Acacia Park, near downtown Colorado Springs. Folks buy locally grown produce directly from the farmer, saving money while pampering the palette. Photo from authors' collection

On 30 August 1980, Memorial Park was the take-off site for the Balloon Race. This photo shows the early morning launch under perfect weather conditions. Ballooning is a popular adventure for many local enthusiasts. Dewey Reinhardt of Colorado Springs attempted to achieve the first balloon crossing of the Atlantic Ocean in 1978; however, uncooperative weather defeated the attempt. Photo courtesy of Gazette Telegraph

*The Springspree '80 Superstars challenge
Lucas Sporting Goods in a fieldball contest
during the city-wide 1981 Springspree
Festival. Photo courtesy of* Gazette
Telegraph

*Springspree is a city-wide celebration held
in June of each year. It features music from
Beethoven to bluegrass, art sales, displays
and contests, awards and races and sports.
Photo courtesy of* Gazette Telegraph

*One of the most unusual events of the
Springspree celebration is the Bed Race,
held through the streets of downtown
Colorado Springs. Bedrunners, sponsored by
local business, push their cargo in a fiercely
contested race to the delight of thousands
who line the course. Photo courtesy of*
Gazette Telegraph

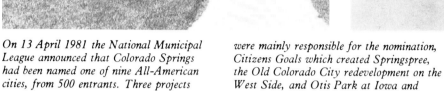

On 13 April 1981 the National Municipal League announced that Colorado Springs had been named one of nine All-American cities, from 500 entrants. Three projects were mainly responsible for the nomination, Citizens Goals which created Springspree, the Old Colorado City redevelopment on the West Side, and Otis Park at Iowa and Dale streets, a park facility designed for handicapped children. These two pictures show Otis Park and the Community Center building. Photo from authors' collection

A daytime photo shows the restored Old Colorado City from Bancroft Park. A visit to this district is a living step back into the early history of this area and makes for a delightful afternoon. Photo from authors' collection

The West Colorado Springs Commercial Club, headed by David Hughes, has restored Old Colorado City to a nostalgic quality. Heightened by a rainy night, the old city brings back memories to old-timers and a sense of historic wonder to all others who pass through the district. A valuable lesson in the need for preservation of historic old buildings is to be learned here. Photo from authors' collection

The growth and expansion of Colorado Springs since 1960 has been phenomenal. The city grew in population from 70,000 to 240,000 and expanded its geographic area from 15.7 square miles to 100.5 square miles. This is the urban sprawl east of Palmer Park, and it shows no sign of slowing down. Photo from authors' collection

This view looks east from the 1981 border between Colorado Springs and the prairie. In a year or two this view will overlook an ocean of houses. Colorado Springs has been among the five fastest growing cities in the United States for the past twenty years. Photo from authors' collection

A 1981 summer view shows Colorado Springs from Palmer Park. The telephoto lens foreshortens the distance: 7,200 foot high Mount Cutler in the upper center is actually eight miles away. Photo from authors' collection

Monument, Colorado, incorporated in 1879, is a small community north from the Air Force Academy. The serenity of this town may soon change forever as it is projected to grow some 256 percent in the next twenty years. The population of the Colorado Springs metropolitan area by that time will exceed a half-million. Photo from authors' collection

Lowell Thomas, a native of Ohio, grew up in Victor, Colorado during the heyday of the goldcamp and graduated from Victor High School. His youthful days were spent selling newspapers, working in the mines (along with boxer Jack Dempsey), reporting for the Victor Daily Record and competing with his rival-friend Ralph Carr who reported for the "other" paper. In this photograph he is sitting beside his high school English teacher, Mabel Barbee Lee, while his one-time rival, now Colorado Governor Ralph Carr stands in the aisle. Mr. Thomas went on to teach English at Princeton University. As a news correspondent he was the first to broadcast from a plane, the first to broadcast from a ship, and the only journalist to interview Lawrence of Arabia. During a lecture in Colorado Springs in August 1981, he reminisced about the three questions he was most often asked, "Where are you coming from? Where are you going now?" and "Where haven't you been?" Mr. Thomas died just a few hours before this writing, 29 August 1981. His delightful Voice of America and So Long will be missed. Photo from authors' collection

Colorado Springs in the 1980s

13 CHAPTER 1981 ~ 1989

The previous twelve chapters of this book were composed on notepads and written for submission to the publisher on a typewriter. This chapter was composed, layed out in a possible format, edited, and printed for submission to the publisher on a PC (that's Personal Computer for those who need to know the computer lingo).

There is no need to detail how much the computer has revolutionized the way America and the world do business. The machine's impact is no less significant than when Gutenburg printed a Bible on the first movable-type press and made books available to everyone, cheaply. It can be argued that Gutenburg's accomplishment was the event which began the Renaissance. Will the accomplishment of the computer begin a new Renaissance, upon which we stand at the threshold?

Colorado Springs has been heavily impacted by the computer. And it has always been a home for the traditions of the Renaissance: knowledge, art and music, games and pleasure . . . and awareness. The city stands now upon a threshold of change and growth in ways known and unseen. At this very moment, the planners who attempt to predict what will be, cannot possibly know how fate will deliver her curve.

A healthy city is a flexible city. Colorado Springs has indeed suffered as the speed-of-light changes in the computer industry have played, sometimes cruelly with her computer industry. There have been companies opening with hope and closing in despair as the world market shifts to attend those who can develop, manufacture, and sell their wares for less. But the city is healthy because it is flexible. Boom and bust doesn't catch Colorado Springs off guard. Are you kidding! On the other side of Pikes Peak, Cripple Creek was once the great metropolis of Colorado. Its hopes, put upon the singular industry of mining, were dashed when panic and metal standards removed its livelihood. Colorado Springs learned! A healthy city is a diverse city.

Colorado Springs is about as diverse as anywhere you can imagine.

What lures people to live in the shadow of Pikes Peak is a nebulous wispy mixture of city and wilderness. In this chapter we have selected from the multitude of offerings, a perspective of some old and new marvels. These may give you an idea about what it is like to live here. Any direction you go from Colorado Springs takes you into a diversely different environment. The mountains which rise so abruptly from the great plain are most magnetic. As John Muir wrote, "Thousands of tired, nerve-shaken, over-civilized people are beginning to find out that going to the mountains is going home; that wildness is a necessity; and that mountain parks and reservations are useful not only as fountains of timber and irrigating rivers, but as fountains of life."

Suburban growth has slowed slightly in the northeast part of the city as new developments occur in the south part of the city, particularly under the eastern flank of 9,565-foot Cheyenne Mountain. Cedar Heights, an exclusive housing development southwest from the Garden of the Gods, was one of the first such developments to be built west of the city. It can be seen from several high vistas in the Garden of the Gods. Crystal Park, below the steep eastern wall of 10,707-foot Cameron's Cone, is not visable from the city below. West of the wealthy Broadmoor area, several developers have built lavish homes and condominiums. As people work to live where they hope to always enjoy the mountain pleasures, they sometimes encounter a reminder of wilderness reality. The lady who rushed out, broom in hand, to chase the dog from her swimming pool was astonished when she realized that the "dog" was a black bear.

In 1979 the Air Force announced that it would build the Consolidated Space Operations Center on the prairie, ten miles east from Colorado Springs. In May

Looking east from the 1980 edge of the city. Photo from authors' collection

Crystal Park. Photo from authors' collection

Development under the shadow of Cheyenne Mountain. Photo from authors' collection

1983 construction began and by September 1985, C-SOC was secure and operational. The Center caused the need for a second parent military project; the newly created Falcon Air Force Base.

Because of the nucleus of secure military operations around Colorado Springs, many important national military projects have been located here. During the period of this chapter, military space operations have been of paramount importance. The Strategic Defense Initiative Organization, whose project has been mis-labelled as "star wars" by some, chose Falcon Air Force Base as the location for its National Test Facility. Computer simulations of possible SDI scenerios are researched, developed, and tested here. In 1988, the Army Space Command was established on the Peterson Air Force Base.

The Colorado Springs Municipal Airport is planning a major construction project. In April 1987, voters authorized a $30 million bond issue to help fund the construction. The facility is expected to cost $76 million. Increased airline operating fees and some federal grant money is expected to pay the difference. The number of passengers embarking from the airport has risen at an annual rate of 12 percent. By 1991, passengers will find a new twelve-gate terminal building, complete with a new runway and taxiways.

There has always been some debate about who discovered the Cave of the Winds. Sketchy documentation holds that "Little Billy" Kimberly, George Snider, Arthur Love, Tom Green, or Charles Cross and the Pickett brothers George and John were the first Anglos to find the cave. Claimed discovery dates range from 1862 to 1880. The Utes and possibly other Native American tribes knew of the cave earlier. According to the story, when chinooks blew across the original entrance pit, the cave "moaned," like a big flute.

Snider explored this and his unchallenged discovery, the Manitou Grand Caverns extensively. But through manipulative business deals after the caves were commercialized in the early 1880s, Snider eventually lost all claims to the cave. Bitterly he wrote and published a booklet about how he discovered and lost the rights to commercialize the cave. In 1907, presumably during the excavation of floor clay in an extention of the commercial section, a passage was found to link the Cave of the Winds and Manitou Grand Caverns.

In 1972 the author, Russ Goodwin, and Lloyd Parris of the National Speleological Society mapped and sur-

The Pines on the Horns of Cheyenne Mountain. Photo from authors' collection

Entrance to Falcon Air Force Base. Photo from authors' collection

veyed the caverns, and discovered a few very beautiful small rooms. The new map showed a large, almost joined loop of passages, with a block of unexplored limestone in between. They predicted more unknown caves would be found in this block. In January 1984, Rick Rhinehart pushed his hand through a "wall" of mud in frustration over an exploratory dig from the Breakdown Room. This discovery of Whale's Belly and Silent Splendor had world-class results. Silent Splendor, contains the finest beaded anthodites and beaded helictites of any cave in the world. Because of its delicacy and uniqueness, Silent Splendor will remain unseen except to cave scientists. Examples of these rare speleothems (formations) can be seen on the commercial tour. But like most show caves, unethical visitors sometimes break off souvenirs, in spite of state law and stiff fines.

During the summer of 1983, Cheyenne Cañon Research studied bristlecone pines on Almagre Mountain, west from Colorado Springs. At timberline, an altitude of 11,600 feet, very near an area where firewood cutting had been allowed, a grove of massive pines were found. The largest have circumferences of over eighteen feet. Samples of wood were cut from fallen trees nearby and

an average growth rate of eighty-nine years per inch (trunk) was established. By measuring diameter, figuring radius and a margin of error due to coriolus effect (an off center middle), it was established the oldest trees could be 3,570 years old; the oldest in Colorado. Coring with a tool would establish absolute age, but the wound can allow rot to damage the heartwood.

Pikes Peak is the dominant peak of its namesake massif. Surrounding it are dozens of lesser peaks, which by themselves would be major mountains in other regions. Almagre Mountain, altitude 12,367 feet, is named for the rosy reddish granite from which it is formed. Each of its major summits has held a microwave station, serving a region larger than Switzerland. To keep such development away from the unique ecology of Pikes Peak, Almagre is used as the "mule." Cheyenne Creek, which headwaters from springs above the reservoir on Almagre, passes through five climate zones during its 6,340-foot altitude drop to end in Fountain Creek, nine miles away. It and its tributaries plunge over many spectacular waterfalls.

In 1962, the Horticultural Arts Society was formed to promote good gardening practices in this region.

Falcon Air Force Base. Photo from authors' collection

Inside the terminal of the Colorado Springs Municipal Airport. Photo from authors' collection

Their demonstration gardens may be seen in Monument Valley Park. HAS conducts classes and workshops, plant sales, a library, an arboretum at the White House Ranch, and opportunities for those interested in gardening to succeed in the arid, capricious climate of the region.

Around the region, gardening climates and soils can vary tremendously. "Banana belts" in the foothill canyons boast fertile soils, more rain and snow, protection from wind and 160+ frost-free summer days. Other areas contend with clay hardpans, scant rain, pelting hailstorms, hurricane chinook winds, and fewer than 80 frost-free summer days. This kind of diversity is tough on gardeners and their art.

Hiking and rock climbing have long been a part of the lure of the Pikes Park region. The Garden of the Gods offers moderate to extremely difficult climbing on variable sandstones. North Cheyenne Canyon, Sentinal and Specimen Rocks, Turkey Rock, and a wealth of alpine crags on Pikes Peak offer many fine routes on variable crystalline granites. The Colorado Mountain Club offers organized hikes and information about climbing instruction. Robert Ormes, a Colorado College professor, wrote the hikers handbook, *Guide to*

the Colorado Rockies, a must for any enthusiast. Stewart Green's *Soft Touch* is a fine guide to the rocks of the Garden of the Gods. Other fine guide books to the peaks, trails, and seasonal mountain activities have been written as during the 1980 decade, more enthusiastic attention than ever focused on mountain activities.

On the west side of Pikes Peaks is Dome Rock State Park, formerly the Mueller Ranch. Some fine granite domes a thousand feet high line a valley where Bighorn sheep from around the region go to breed. The Nature Conservancy was active in the creation and study of this park. While walk-up routes exist on the back of the domes, the peeling-onion granite makes for some hazardous and extremely difficult rock climbing.

Ski Broadmoor is one of the smallest ski areas in Colorado. While it receives some roasting from many local "fryers," it is a unique and very diverse little area. The single "main" slope has only a 600-foot vertical drop. But on that run one can ski moguls, powder (after a big snow), flats, a piste (trough), and test sharp ski edges on the ski area's famous ice.

Ski Broadmoor was the first Colorado ski area to manufacture some of its snow. During the drought of

Beaded anthodites and helictites encrust a group of stalactites in Silent Splendor. Photo courtesy Cave of the Winds

Perhaps the finest spray of beaded helictites in the world, some measuring two feet in length. Photo courtesy Cave of the Winds

One of the most fantastic speleothems in the world. Photo courtesy Cave of the Winds

227

Perhaps the oldest tree in Colorado, a 3,000+ year old bristlecone pine on Almagre Mountain. Photo courtesy CCR

1976-77, other Colorado ski areas learned about the advantage of man-made snow, and now most begin their seasons with or without "Mother Nature."

The Ski Broadmoor ski school is one of the best in Colorado and the racing program has produced some extremely fine racers, some of whom have made the U.S. Ski Team. Formerly a finger of the Broadmoor, the ski area is now under the management of the City of Colorado Springs Park and Recreation Department.

During the early part of the 1980s, the Pikes Peak Ski Area, with the help of several enthusiastic owners and promoters, tried to upgrade its image in order to remain competitive. However costly improvements and several lean snow years proved to be deadly for business. Pikes Peak generally receives less snow than the central mountains, which absorb remaining Pacific moisture. The upslope "Albuquerque low" often drops more moisture along the foot of the great peak than on its alpine slopes.

Since the arrival of the Olympic Training Center (OTC) and the National Sports Festivals, athletic activity in Colorado Springs has focused and intensified, especially in less known events. For years the Broadmoor World Arena has trained ice skating champions.

Christine Haigler Krall, who grew up and trained at the World Arena, was a member of the 1964 Olympic and World figure skating teams. Now a successful skating coach, her daughters Lindsay, Katie, and Abbey continue their family tradition. Skaters who hope to compete internationally, train for many long, daily hours from morning until night. Youngsters have specially modified schooling or tutoring. Their schedule demands leave little time for personal recreation.

What is now considered the finest velodrome in the United States was built in Memorial Park and is part of the OTC. The 1986 World Cycling Championships were held here. Track racing, like criterium racing, is very much a team competition and pre-race strategy is intensely considered by the cyclists.

While popular sports need no explanation, there are many Olympic events which are less popular, but glamorous, exacting, and requisite of extreme conditioning and skill. The governing bodies of many of these events are based at the OTC, where their athletes study and train. Volleyball has received more national attention and both mens and womens national teams have been very successful. Flo Hyman, the extraordinary Olympic player who died of a rare heart disease, trained and is now memorialized at the OTC.

Almagre Mountain. Photo from authors' collection

Horticultural Arts Society Demonstration Garden. Photo from authors' collection

Josephine Falls, best seen in early summer, is the highest and one of the prettiest waterfalls on a tributary of Cheyenne Creek. Photo from authors' collection

The garden of Cheyenne Cañon Research features conifers. A giant sequoia planted here in 1977 grows thirty-five inches per annum. If it survives in your children's lifetime it wil be the tallest and biggest tree in Colorado. CCR has researched and is growing many other rare and difficult conifers, including Torrey pine, Coulter pine, Alerce and many cypresses. Photo from authors' collection

The fantastic mobile garden of sculptor Starr Kempf must rank among the most unusual in the world. During the 1980 decade, his growing garden of wind-motored sculptures has gained fame by word of mouth and slows down every passer-by in amazement. The garden will be donated to the city following the sculptor's wishes, where it will become part of Cheyenne Canyon Park. Photo from authors' collection

The minor league baseball drought in Colorado Springs ended when in late 1987 the Hawaii Islanders club moved to Colorado Springs and became the Colorado Springs Sky Sox, a farm club of the Cleveland Indians. After spring training in Tucson, Arizona, the team will play about seventy home games in Sky Sox Stadium, and as many road games as members of the Pacific Coast League. So far the young team has drawn much fan enthusiasm and support, averaging three thousand spectators per game in Colorado Springs and growing.

"At last, a hall in which *I* can hear too!" said one of the players of the orchestra. The El Pomar Hall of the Pikes Peak Center is rapidly being recognized as one of the premier symphony halls in America. While some grumbled about it being "Ansbacher's Barn," during construction, what a barn it is! The hall has a wonderful stage and has now hosted many of the world's greatest musicians and dancers, and is home to the Colorado Springs Symphony Orchestra.

And *that* orchestra is recognized as one of the best regional orchestras in the world. Conductor laureate Charles Ansbacher has retired his baton, as the

The garden of Mrs. Peggy Parr often slows down the traffic. She spent many years developing one of the finest private perennial gardens. From May until October frost, her garden of Hemerocallis, Delphinium, Iris, numerous composites, and other flowers bursts with wonderful color. Like the other gardens, this one uses less water than conventional lawns; a blessing to water conservation. Photo from authors' collection

A climber approaches an overhang on Specimen Rock. Photo from authors' collection

orchestra enters a new era under the leadership of Maestro Christopher Wilkins.

The Colorado Springs Chorale, a 120-voice auditioned choir, performs great choral literature, often in association with the Colorado Springs Symphony Orchestra, several times during the season. Maestro Donald P. Jenkins is a wizard who seems to use magic to generate stunningly musical performances. In 1984 the Chorale sang Handel's *Messiah*, a traditional public demand. But in order to create a fresh interpretation, they sang it *from memory!*

The Colorado Opera Festival has been under the heavy financial stress which has recently silenced so many performing arts organizations in America. In 1987, financial pressures loomed and it became clear that unless they were resolved, the opera festival would close. But close work between musicians, management, and creditors since has for now, saved the festival.

The population center of Colorado Springs continues to drift northeast. Technically the downtown is now near the western edge of the city. Population estimate of Colorado Springs is 275,000 people with perhaps another 100,000 people in the whole metropolitan area.

Much of the downtown is recognizable to the "old timer." But many changes have taken place too. New

A dizzying tyrolean traverse on the Demonstration Pinnacle. Photo from authors' collection

Hikers cautiously approach Spoon Falls on Buffalo Creek. Photo courtesy Carol Hetzler

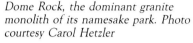

Dome Rock, the dominant granite monolith of its namesake park. Photo courtesy Carol Hetzler

buildings in the downtown core reflect an influx of major financial interest.

When General Palmer's surveyors plotted out the streets of the new town, they were directed to make them a hundred feet wide. Palmer, in his typical foresighted manner, thought that one day there would be a need for such wide streets. As the city grew, and especially when automobiles and buses became the principal locomotion, the wide streets became blessings.

When the Plaza of the Rockies, a new downtown office center was built, some controversy was stirred up. For some, it represented the upward financial growth of the city and was an architecturally beautiful building. No doubts about that. But it also consumed part of Tejon Street, forcing a traffic reroute and spoiling the street plan laid out by General Palmer. It represents a battleground between "oldtimers" who demand preservation and "newcomers" who demand growth.

South from Colorado Springs in Rock Creek Canyon is the May Natural History Museum. It features one of the world's finest exhibits of giant insects; the life work of James May. Thousands of huge beetles, phasmids, moths and butterflies, and spiders from every jungle on earth can be seen here.

James' father was an explorer and naturalist for the British Museum (Natural History), researching snakes, orchids, and lizards, and died of yellow fever while on the Amazon. Ted May, a brother, helped create the entomological exhibit for the National Museum of Brazil in Rio de Janiero. James' young life story could be an "Indiana Jones" movie.

In 1947, James and his son John founded the permanent museum in Colorado Springs. In 1949 about 10 percent of the collection was exhibited in the Woolworth store downtown, taking up the entire building.

In 1988 the affiliate National Museum of Photography opened, featuring some of the finest American photography with particular emphasis on space. Founder Bill Purdom and the May family plan to expand the museums into a network which could become one of the great museum centers of the world.

Storms in the Pikes Peak region can be violent. Pikes Peak and the Palmer Divide are barriers which often create weather patterns unique to the region. It can snow in Denver and be clear in Colorado Springs, or vice versa. Sometimes thunderstorms occur. On 19 July 1985, a thunderstorm which dropped almost six inches of rain on the west side of the city in a two hour period

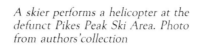
A skier does a parallel turn on the moguled upper part of "main" at Ski Broadmoor. Photo from authors' collection

A skier performs a helicopter at the defunct Pikes Peak Ski Area. Photo from authors'collection

Christine Haigler Krall and daughters. Photo courtesy Christine Haigler Krall

A cyclist rides the stripes, practicing technique on the OTC Velodrome. Photo from authors'collection

233

A public tour watches hopeful future Olympians in a practice volleyball scrimmage. Photo from authors' collection

Dwight Taylor safely touches base for the Colorado Springs Sky Sox. Photo courtesy Ernie Ferguson

washed out the Gold Camp Road. These storms rapidly turn the splashing mountain streams into deadly raging torrents.

A phenomena called the "Albuquerque low," produces most of the precipitation in the region. Low pressure to the south draws moisture from the Gulf of Mexico, which drops as rain or snow when it meets the Front Range barrier. On 14-15 January 1987, a snowstorm dropped forty-three inches of snow on the western part of the city. During such storms, the National Weather Service usually records lesser amounts of precipitation because that station is east of the city, on the drier prairie.

The winters are extremely diverse. Nothing is typical. This record by is from January 1983.

Date:	Jan 8	Jan 9	Jan 10	Jan 11	Jan 12	Jan 13
High: (F)	43	53	21	43	22	29
Low: (F)	-7	20	6	4	18	10
Snow	0	1″	0	1″	2″	0
Wind (MPH)	9	45	12	9	18	15
Day	Clr	Cdy	Clr	Cdy	Cdy	Clr

Date:	Jan 14	Jan 15	Jan 16	Jan 17	Jan 18
High: (F)	50	44	14	67	55
Low: (F)	15	28	0	7	29
Snow	0	2″	0	0	0
Wind (MPH)	28	25	8	100+	56
Day	Clr	Cdy	Clr	Clr	Clr

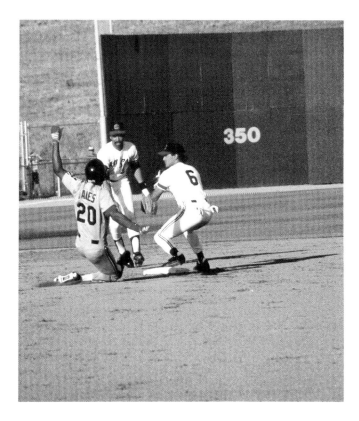

Tommy Hinzo and Brian Giles connect
for a double play at Sky Sox Stadium.
Photo courtesy Ernie Ferguson

"Among the immortal dreams of boys. . . . "
Photo courtesy Ernie Ferguson

Christopher Wilkins. Photo courtesy
Colorado Springs Symphony Orchestra

An orchestra musician's view of the
El Pomar Great Hall of the Pikes Peak
Center. Photo courtesy Ollie Wicks

The Colorado Springs Chorale on the
stage of the El Pomar Great Hall. Photo
courtesy Colorado Springs Chorale

Colorado Springs is well endowed with city parks. The most splendid are the mountain parks; Garden of the Gods, Cheyenne Canyon, Bear Creek Canyon, and Palmer Park. These provide the necessity quoted by Muir at the beginning of this chapter.

Encroachment by development, misuse and overuse by the public, and vandalism have become major issues around these areas. During the 1975-85 period, destruction proliferated in all of the mountain parks. Trail erosion, painted graffiti, animal and plant destruction, vandalism and violent crimes, beyond the watchful eyes of police, reached critical stages.

In the early 1980s, thousands of acres of conifers between 8,000 and 10,000 feet altitude began losing leaves and many are now dead. Research indicates air pollution and acid rain are major factors. Loss of alpine vegetation, particularly in the canyons, will produce conditions for disastrous floods like those of 1921 and 1935.

The city management is responding with studies of the parks, and have taken steps to restore damaged park areas and protect remaining pristine sections. The challenge of defining the purpose for the mountain parks and controlling activities incompatible with their wildness will be a chief environmental issue of the 1990s.

Some of the bristlecone pines on Almagre Mountain may have been alive when Pikes Peak's cirques still had glaciers in them. Here, the whole witness of civilization on the plain below is recorded on little more than an inch of wood.

The whole witness of that civilization is recorded on these pages from a perspective of people who represent the most recent two of five native generations.

Enough cannot be written about Colorado Springs. Like any metropolis, it has some problems. But the quality of life here includes many wonders which far outweigh the problems. The next generation, enrolled in local and foreign schools, have a responsibility to learn about why Colorado Springs is so special, if they want to live here and enjoy it. Schools do an efficient job of instruction. But education is underfunded and modern American society seems to want the schools to raise its children as well as teach them, with little assistance. Colorado Springs, like its native country has reached a crossroads. In a time when the prosperity of good life blesses all, we must remember that we are not the last people. Those who ignore the children produce the gangs which seek identity through crime. The society who pays attention to its children preserves its treasures, its heritage, and prosperity.

It is all history.

Pikes Peaks Avenue and Tejon Street on a typical August day in downtown Colorado Springs. Photo from authors' collection

Looking south on Tejon Street toward the Plaza of the Rockies. Photo from the authors' collection

John May. Photo courtesy May Museum

Ornithoptera butterflies, the world's largest and most spectacular, collected by the Mays in New Guinea. Photo courtesy May Museum

Giant phasmids from the New Guinea jungles. The center specimen is eighteen inches long. Photo courtesy May Museum

*May Natural History Museum. Photo
courtesy May Museum*

*Cheyenne Creek, two days after the big
rain of 19 July 1985. Photo from authors'
collection*

*This storm on 7 August 1989 again
washed out the Gold Camp Road. Photo
from authors' collection*

City workers removing tons of scree which closed North Cheyenne Canyon after the 7 August 1989 storm. Photo from authors' collection

Graffiti vandalism at St. Mary's Falls trailhead. Photo from authors' collection

A 35-inch snowfall on 14-15 October 1985 spoiled the fall colors. Photo from authors' collection

Garden of the Gods and Pikes Peak.
Photo from authors' collection

Upper North Cheyenne Canyon and
large patches of acid rain/pollution
ravaged forest. Photo from authors'
collection

Helen Hunt Falls during a rare autumn
fog. Photo courtesy Carol Hetzler

Profiles
in
Leadership

Cities are in large part a reflection of the quality and success of their economic and cultural institutions and the people who manage them.

From the earliest times Colorado Springs has been blessed with people and institutions of foresight and tenacity. Their collective story is reflected in the preceding pages. The detailed stories of some of the best are told in the following pages.

The Publisher

Colorado Springs Pioneers Museum

Colorado Springs Pioneers Museum

The Colorado Springs Pioneers Museum, located in the historic 1903 El Paso County Courthouse, makes the history of the Pikes Peak region come alive in exhibits emphasizing the unique character of this uncommon frontier community. As the focal point of lovely downtown Colorado Springs, the museum draws thousands of people into the city annually. The elegant courthouse centered in one of two primary downtown parks, is surrounded by inviting green lawns, colorful blooming flowers, and a splendid granite fountain.

In 1896, a group of pioneers interested in preserving the memorabilia of the Pikes Peak region formed the El Paso County Pioneers Association. They first displayed their collection in the El Paso County Courthouse in 1909. The display continued through 1937, when the city of Colorado Springs approved municipal support, creating the Pioneers Museum.

The Museum was housed for many years at 25 West Kiowa Street until overcrowding prompted the use of the El Paso County Courthouse again to house the collections. After entering the building on the National Register of Historic Places, the Museum re-opened its doors in the new location in 1979, following a successful "Move the Museum" fundraising drive. Since that time the building restoration has progressed at a steady pace.

Guided by a mission to collect, preserve, and interpret the history and culture of the Pikes Peak region, the Museum features permanent exhibits on the history

of the area and changing exhibits on topics of local and national interest. Popular traveling shows of quilts, historic photographs, aviation, Native American culture, and art pottery complement an active changing exhibition schedule which has included everything from juke boxes and spacecraft to Western art and Victorian underwear.

Public programs range from scholarly presentations to family festivals. The Museum has been host to a variety of events: lectures on the American cowboy, Hispanic celebrations, antique auto shows, firefighters demonstrations, and displays of Harley Davidson motorcycles.

The Museum operates an historic reference library and archives, the Starsmore Center for Historical Research, which concentrates on materials relating to the Pikes Peak region. Included in these collections are: the Cragin collection; General William Jackson Palmer's personal papers; photographic portraits of early pioneers; newspaper clippings; city directories from the 1870s; and many old diaries, scrapbooks, and photo albums. These materials are used by the public for genealogical purposes, research papers, and school projects.

The Museum has an active community outreach program and provides tours, speakers, presentations for schools, and other special programs. With a dedicated group of volunteer docents, the Museum provides tours for over eight thousand people annually, more than seven thousand of which are school children. Attendance, which numbers approximately 100,000 annually, continues to rise as the Museum gains in popularity

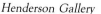

Henderson Gallery   Main Courtroom

and in national prominence.

The Colorado Springs Pioneers Museum offers a rewarding and enjoyable experience for people of all ages. A visit provides a look into the spirit, past and present, of the city nestled at the foot of Pikes Peak, America's most famous mountain.

Hewlett-Packard Company

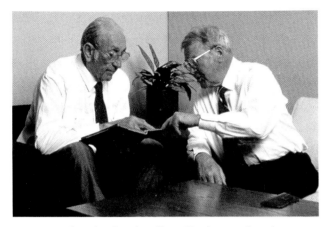

David Packard and William Hewlett, co-founders

The Hewlett-Packard Company was formed in 1939 as a partnership between William Hewlett and David Packard, fellow electrical engineering students at Stanford University. They founded the company on the beliefs that people are committed to doing a good job and that, given the opportunity, they can make sound decisions in their areas of responsibility and carry out those decisions to benefit the company.

Headquartered in Palo Alto, California, Hewlett-Packard facilities are concentrated in California, Colorado, the Northeast, and Pacific Northwest. In Colorado, Hewlett-Packard employs over eight thousand people, with facilities in five communities along the front range: Loveland, Fort Collins, Greeley, Englewood, and Colorado Springs. It was natural to select Colorado as a location since Pueblo was David Packard's birthplace, and because his parents had graduated from Colorado College.

Hewlett-Packard began manufacturing in Loveland in 1959 and the Colorado Springs division followed closely behind in 1962, when the company transferred its oscilloscope design and manufacturing operation from California. Today the division designs, manufactures, and markets digitizing oscilloscopes and logic analyzers.

As a result of demand for custom-packaged integrated circuits, the Colorado Springs Tech Center was formed in 1978. This entity of Hewlett-Packard provides custom circuits to company divisions around the world.

Colorado Telecommunications Division (CTD), operating in Colorado Springs since 1981, produces data communications test equipment to solve communications problems. Divided into Local Area Networking (LAN) and Wide Area Networking (WAN) testing needs, CTD offers a family of protocol analyzers with an array of solutions for identifying data communication problems.

Formed in 1982, Logic Systems Division is responsible for state-of-the-art microprocessor development systems. These systems are used by engineering and scientific customers to design products using embedded microprocessors. A spinoff of the division, the Electronic Design Division, is involved in the Computer-Aided Engineering (CAE) systems and Computer-Aided Design (CAD) systems for electronic circuitry and printed circuit board development.

Being one of the largest employers in Colorado Springs, Hewlett-Packard takes pride in its community involvement. This active role of outreach is accomplished with volunteers helping with the concerns of the public sector, especially addressing the social and educational needs of the community. Programs such as the United Way and Junior Achievement are greatly enhanced by the contributions of time and money from company employees and the community. The company is also committed to the educational needs of its employees. This is evidenced by the tuition reimbursement programs offered to employees, as well as the company's commitment to work with local colleges and universities to enhance their programs in the high tech area.

Hewlett-Packard provides the tools to harness the power of information, instruments to make precise measurements, a range of powerful computers, and peripheral products. These help to analyze, manage, and store information, graphics and printing capabilities, and networking and software to link it all together. These capabilities, combined with a commitment to quality and customer satisfaction, give Hewlett-Packard a solid foundation for future innovation and growth.

KRDO AM/FM/TV

KRDO AM/FM/TV—the only locally, family-owned and operated radio and television station in Colorado, and one of the few remaining in the country—is the story of one man: Harry W. Hoth.

In 1947, just after KRDO-AM was founded, Hoth became a part-time salesman. Just seven years later Hoth bought KRDO and became president and general manager of the radio station. His vision has guided KRDO throughout the years, making it a community involved company known for its quality programming and comprehensive news coverage.

KRDO-AM began operation on March 15, 1947, from the first floor of the Alta Vista Hotel in the 100 block of North Cascade Avenue. A spirit of local pride for an energetic and growing community set the pace for KRDO-AM programming during the early years. The Pikes Peak Hill Climb, the oldest auto race in the country, was broadcast for the first time on KRDO. The last run of the Midland Terminal Railroad from Cripple Creek to Colorado Springs was described from the engine of old No. 59. Regular remote dance programs were carried from the Broadmoor Tavern and KRDO origi-nated many programs for the Columbine Network, a group of Colorado stations. When the disastrous fire of 1949 swept up the slope of Cheyenne Mountain, rav-aging Camp Carson, KRDO became the main com-munications hub for the city and the nation. Constant remote broadcasts from all areas were fed to many Colo-rado stations and to two national networks.

In 1953, the cramped quarters of the Alta Vista Hotel gave way to a new facility at 399 South 8th Street, and that same year, on September 21, KRDO-TV signed on the air with the opening of the World Series, as the New York Yankees took on the Brooklyn Dodgers. KRDO-TV, having recently celebrated its thirty-fifth anniversa-ry, has since pioneered many broadcasts of local events including parades, street breakfasts, graduations, the Colorado State Fair, election results, and high school football and basketball games. Because of these remote broadcasts, the transmitting facilities were moved to the top of Cheyenne Mountain, making KRDO the first station to give full coverage to Pueblo. With the subse-

Harry W. Hoth, President and Chief Executive Officer

quent purchase of the first TV Mobile Unit in southern Colorado, KRDO could directly broadcast from anywhere in the area.

KRDO-TV is a station of many firsts. It was first with televised coverage of the Pikes Peak Hill Climb; first with live pictures from the top of Pikes Peak; first with color and portable video tape machines; first with a translator system to broadcast to cities and towns in the mountains of southern Colorado; and first with electronic news gathering equipment for its newsroom.

With its dedicated and professional staff of anchors, reporters, and photographers, KRDO News 13 continues to be a leader in the field by offering award-winning reporting, in-depth series, special weekly features, and a sports department that is unsurpassed in southern Colorado. This excellence in broadcast journalism was recognized when KRDO-News 13 captured the 1988 Emmy for Best Newscast in southern Colorado.

KRDO-TV 13 produces a wide variety of local programs, covering such events as the U.S. Air Force Academy graduation, the KRDO Triple Crown of Running, the Pikes Peak Rodeo Parade, the Colorado State Fair, the Junior Livestock Sale, and the National High School Rodeo finals. Also produced are two weekly programs: "Scene 13," which examines local current events, and "Emphasis on Arts," an award-winning program on the arts in southern Colorado.

For its production of the "Pikes Peak Marathon Show," KRDO won the prestigious IRIS award, presented by the National Association of Television Program Executives, in recognition of excellence in local programming.

KRDO-FM began broadcasting in October 1969, making KRDO unique in the Colorado Springs market—the only company with a television station and an AM and FM station. The format for 95.1 KRDO-FM is contemporary easy listening. This popular blend of instrumentals and vocals has consistently made KRDO-FM one of the top three stations in the market. AM 1240 KRDO, "Colorado's Gold," is affiliated with the Satellite Music Network, and features oldies from the fifties, sixties, and seventies.

In 1985, Harry Hoth was named Colorado "Broadcaster of the Year" by the Colorado Broadcasters Association, the second time he has earned the honor. Throughout his career, Hoth has been instrumental in community affairs, serving both as a government official and a community leader. He served two terms as mayor of Colorado Springs from 1963 to 1967 and a total of nineteen years on the Colorado Springs City Council and City Planning Commission. Additionally, his dynamic and spirited community involvement is exemplified by his support of organizations and programs which benefit young people.

Memorial Hospital

Founded in 1904, Memorial Hospital built a new building in 1911 at the site of the hospital's present location on Boulder Street.

Memorial Hospital has provided health care to the people of Colorado Springs since the turn of the century.

Founded in 1904 by the Woman's Home Missionary Society of the Methodist Church, Memorial was originally named the Colorado Conference Deaconness Hospital. The three-story structure, with thirty beds, was located on the east side of Institute Street.

As the city grew, the need for health care grew with it. Plans for a new, larger building began in 1907. The founder of Colorado Springs, William J. Palmer, agreed to donate the land at Memorial's present site, the 1400 block of east Boulder. In 1909, the cornerstone of the new two-story, cream-colored building was laid. In 1911, the new facility opened with a new name—Beth-El Hospital.

In 1943, the Methodist Church decided to sell the hospital, and following a vote by the city council, the city of Colorado Springs purchased the institution. As a tribute to those who died in World War II, the hospital was renamed Memorial. The city council appointed a Board of Trustees to oversee the hospital, a practice that continues today.

Today, Memorial is a dynamic health care leader for all of Southern Colorado. Memorial offers specialized services in cardiology (including open heart surgery); pediatrics; cancer treatment; emergency and trauma services for children and adults; sophisticated maternity services for before, during, and after the baby arrives, include perinatology and neonatology for high risk pregnancies and high risk newborns. The Intensive Care Nursery provides the highest level of care for critically-ill infants and Memorial offers the only Pediatric Inten-sive Care Unit in southern Colorado.

In addition to having the finest facilities and the most qualified personnel, Memorial pursues a commitment to use the latest in technology. Magnetic resonance imaging, CT scanning, and hyperbaric oxygen chambers attest to this commitment.

Memorial Hospital, one of Colorado Springs' major employers, seeks involvement in the community beyond patient care. In addition to extensive community health education, a wide variety of health screenings, information, and counseling, the hospital offers educational opportunities for health careers in radiological technology and nursing.

Memorial also sponsors special programs for today's patient needs, such as the "Lighten up for Life" weight control program, the Women's Center, the Pediatric After Hours Clinic, the 50+ program and the Cholesterol Center.

In addition, Memorial operates both Health Network, a health maintenance organization, and Medical Network, a preferred provider organization, which offer health insurance benefits to employers and employees in a cost effective manner.

Taking seriously its designation as the hospital that belongs to the people of Colorado Springs, Memorial will continue to provide the highest level of health care to its citizens.

Memorial Hospital, a 300 bed acute care, general hospital, provides many highly specialized services to the people of Colorado Springs.

Association of Graduates–USAF Academy

*Proposed Association of Graduates
Headquarters/Alumni House.*

The Association of Graduates (AOG) of the United States Air Force Academy, Inc., is the alumni organization serving the Academy and its graduates. The need for such an association was recognized by Academy officials even prior to the graduation of the first class in 1959. It was not until 1965, however, that formal organization took place. The original objectives of the association, since broadened, included acquiring, preserving, and disseminating historical materials relating to the institution and its graduates, as well as encouraging and fostering the study of air and space science. In 1968, the fledgling alumni group sought and received certification as a nonprofit, Colorado corporation. Granted tax–exempt status by the Colorado and federal governments as a charitable and educational organization, the AOG has since matured into a multi–faceted association providing a wide variety of services and support to members and their *alma mater.*

The association proudly acknowledges the support of some thirteen thousand dues-paying graduate and associate members. Included in the latter category are cadets; cadet and graduate parents; corporations; Academy faculty and staff members; and other friends of the Academy and the association.

An association office staff of nine carries out all service and support operations. The AOG serves its members via publication of a quarterly magazine, *Checkpoints,* and the annual *Register of Graduates.* Additionally, members may purchase Academy and AOG memorabilia and take advantage of an affinity MasterCard; an unsecured line of credit; discounted hotel, rental car, and airline services; and locator information. The association also plays an important role as the repository of historical and biographical data on all Academy graduates. All reunion and homecoming activities are coordinated by the AOG staff.

The association's ever–growing support of the Academy and the Air Force now includes postgraduate scholarships; sponsorship of lectures, seminars, and symposia; administration of memorial funds and programs; and management of numerous endowment funds established to support continuing Academy programs. The AOG has also assumed a major fund–raising role in support of the Academy. Recognizing that federal funds are continuously scarce, the association initiated and continues to administer the annual Air Force Academy (AFA) Fund. Tax–deductible contributions to the AFA Fund are subsequently gifted by the AOG to the Academy to support a variety of priority cadet enrichment programs to provide "the extra margin of excellence."

The Association of Graduates has come a long way since its board members met in the basements of their homes. While continuing to occupy temporary offices at the Academy, anticipated expansion dictates the need for a permanent headquarters/alumni house. A major fund–raising campaign is now under way, and the association looks forward to occupying its own facility on the Academy grounds and to continuing service to the institution and its graduates.

Sherman & Howard

Ben Wendelken

In 1937, J. Hartley Murray (1911-1983), William Baker, and Ben Wendelken formed the firm of Murray, Baker & Wendelken, in what came to be one of the most respected firms in Colorado Springs.

Through the years, Murray, Baker & Wendelken became a strong force in the legal community, both as a group and individually. Mr. Murray graduated from Colorado College in 1933 and from the University of Colorado School of Law in Boulder in 1936. He was awarded a Bronze Star for his participation in the Nuremberg trials, and received several distinctions during his law career, including being inducted as a fellow in the American College of Trial Lawyers in 1963, one of the highest honors in American jurisprudence, and as a fellow in the American College of Probate Counsel in 1974. He is a past president of the Colorado and El Paso County Bar associations.

William Baker graduated from the University of Colorado in 1935 and from the University of Colorado Law School at Boulder in 1937. After a stint in the Navy in World War II where he worked in intelligence, he joined Mr. Murray and Mr. Wendelken as an associate in 1937, becoming a partner a few years later. Through the years, he was very active in the community, acting as director of the chamber of commerce, and as president of the Cheyenne School district, the El Paso

County Bar Association, and the Winter Nightclub, a lecture organization. He remains active in the firm, practicing probate, trust, estate administration, and real estate law.

Ben Wendelken has practiced law since 1925. One of the more legendary successes in his long and distinguished legal career occurred in 1933 when he went up against one of the most powerful figures in Colorado Springs—and won. Spencer Penrose had refused to pay a toll to Charlie Ryan, a highway guard, for traveling by the Corley Mountain Highway near Old Stage Road. A scuffle ensued, and Mr. Penrose charged that Ryan used a crowbar against him. Wendelken defended Ryan successfully in court, then sued Penrose for false imprisonment. Mr. Penrose was so impressed with the brash young Wendelken that he sent some of his legal business to Wendelken's law firm, including representation of the El Pomar Foundation and the Broadmoor Hotel.

In 1984, the firm merged with the Denver law firm of Sherman & Howard. Sherman & Howard is the oldest law firm in Colorado, founded by James H. Pershing in 1892, the year that the cornerstone was laid in the

William Baker

State Capitol Building. Mr. Pershing represented the city and county of Denver in connection with the development of its water resources and was a prominent advocate of the importance of capital formation to the growth of the West.

The merger of Sherman & Howard and Murray, Baker & Wendelken increased the firm's ability to provide specialized legal services to clients in Colorado Springs and throughout southern Colorado. Since that time, the firm has experienced substantial growth in its practice, and has continually expanded its staff and facilities to meet the needs of its growing clientele.

Throughout its history, the firm has had within its walls the lawyers responsible for making much of Colorado's legal history, lawyers capable of drawing on first-

J. Hartley Murray

hand knowledge of events and developments spanning many decades—lawyers such as Hartley Murray, William Baker, and Ben Wendelken. It is committed to providing these benefits to all of its clients.

The fifteen lawyers in the Colorado Springs office include members of the firm's business, employment law, litigation, real estate, and tax and probate departments. In addition, the firm's government contracts practice is based in the Colorado Springs office. The Colorado Springs lawyers regularly work with lawyers in the firms other regional offices in Denver, Albuquerque, Santa Fe, and Reno, assisting clients throughout the Rocky Mountain region as their needs require.

MAXCOR Manufacturing, Inc.

MAXCOR owners, from left to right, are Don Werschky, Ron Marold, Jack Head, and Bob Werschky.

MAXCOR is a long time Colorado Springs manufacturer of precision components used in computer disk drives, photocopy machines, and high speed laser printers. The company was formed in October 1981, by the merger of two companies, Proto Shop Automatics and Colorado Springs Machine Corporation. Prior to the merger, Colorado Springs Machine Corporation had been in operation for over thirty years and Proto Shop for sixteen years. Both of MAXCOR's predecessor companies were founded by people in the machinist trade who had a strong desire to form their own independent business based on quality of workmanship and service to American business. Independence and the dream of owning their own business were strong motivating factors.

Colorado Springs Machine Corporation was founded in 1947. At that time the four employees specialized in designing and building tools, dies, and special machines for the limited number of large manufacturing companies in the Colorado area. The original location was 7 East Cucharras Street. In 1952, Carl P. Werschky purchased controlling interest in the company and immediately began plans for a new building at 4400 (now renumbered 4230) North Nevada Avenue. This building still exists and is part of the MAXCOR complex on North Nevada Avenue. Employment has grown from seven in 1947, to eighty-five in 1981, when the merger occurred.

Proto Shop was founded on July 3, 1965, when Larry Norberg, Larry Ashcroft, and Jack Head purchased an existing business having assets of four pieces of equipment, a mill, lathe, drill press, and cut off saw, all contained in a nine hundred square foot building. One year later, Norberg and Head bought Ashcroft's interest and moved the business to a five thousand square foot building at 601 West Cucharras. Ron Marold bought an interest in Proto Shop March 1, 1967. In the fall of 1969, Proto Shop moved to a building at 3020 North Stone Street. Larry Norberg died in October 1970, leaving Ron Marold and Jack Head as the remaining owners. The company continued to grow and had 135 employees at the time of the merger in 1981.

Major production now is precision mechanical parts and assemblies requiring high technology, and which compete in the world marketplace. However, products have changed over the years. In the early days, Colorado Springs Machine Corporation specialized in tools, dies, and special machines for production. Later jobs included parts for space craft and for the nuclear energy programs at Los Alamos and Sandia laboratories. Parts were made for Lunar and Martian landers. The Viking Martian Lander contained a microdot photograph of the signatures of fourteen CSMC people who worked on that project. Proto Shop, on the other hand, specialized in larger scale production of machined parts and assemblies. In 1970, Proto Shop began vacuum heat treating, a modern technology that was not available elsewhere in the Rocky Mountain area. MAXCOR continues to provide vacuum and other types of heat treating services.

As MAXCOR enters the 1990s, employment has risen to over three hundred, buildings are located on Stone Street and Nevada Avenue, and plans are underway to add another thirty-six thousand square feet of manufacturing and office space.

Kraemer and Kendall, P. C.

Phillip A. Kendall and Sandy F. Kraemer have practiced law together in Colorado Springs since 1969. While their educational backgrounds are similar, they did not meet until after law school. They share a common philosophy of seeking to provide the highest quality of legal services within the framework of a small to medium size firm. This structure has allowed the firm to deliver a wide range of legal services to many long-term clients, while limiting administrative time and expense, and allowing each firm attorney to maximize his or her own professional interests and abilities.

Kraemer and Kendall emphasizes real estate, estate planning and estates, civil litigation and business planning. Increasing attention is being placed on developing client legal and business strategies and entrepreneurial objectives.

Sandy F. Kraemer received his B.S. in engineering from Stanford University in 1959 and did graduate work in 1960. He received his *Juris Doctor* from the University of Colorado in 1963. He was a founder and past president of the Colorado Springs Estate Planning Council and instructor in real estate and estate planning courses. He has served as committee chairman at world conferences of the World Peace Through Law organization in Madrid and Berlin. He is the author of *Solar Law: Present and Future with Proposed Forms,* and numerous published legal articles.

Phillip A. Kendall received his B.S. in engineering from Stanford University in 1964. He studied one year at the University of Freiburg in Germany and received his *Juris Doctor* from the University of Colorado in 1969. In 1977, he was selected as the Outstanding Young Lawyer by the Young Lawyer's section of the Colorado Bar Association. He has served as a trustee of the El Paso County Bar Association and on the Board of Governors of the Colorado Bar Association. He is a member of the National Health Lawyers Association and the Colorado Springs Estate Planning Council. He is also a member of the Board of Directors of the United Bank of Colorado Springs.

John S. Benson, the third member in the firm, received his B.A. in political science at Vanderbilt University in 1969, *magna cum laude, Phi Beta Kappa,* and his *Juris Doctor* from the University of Virginia. He received the highest score on the Florida Bar Exam in July 1974, and gained extensive civil law experience as a partner in a major firm in Jacksonville before moving to Colorado. Since 1985, he has served as a member of the Board of Directors of one of the nation's largest warehousing and distribution companies.

Kraemer and Kendall encourages pursuit and development of community and personal interests to balance

From left to right are Pauline Roberts, John S. Benson, Nancy Chadwick, Phillip A. Kendall, Lana Kushinsky, Sandy F. Kraemer and Shirley R. Hair.

work. Phil has tackled an English Channel swim and triathlons. He moved from chairing the Board of Directors of the Colorado Springs Symphony to chairing the successful Pikes Peak Center project, which raised over $7 million in private funding to build the downtown Performing Arts Center. He just completed a six-year term on the Board of Trustees for Penrose Hospitals. After chairing Project 2000, he became chairman of the recent effort to build a downtown sports arena.

Sandy was twice elected to the University of Colorado Board of Regents and served as chairman of the board. He served on the Colorado Springs Charter Review Commission and was named Colorado "Conversationist of the Year" for his work as chairman of the Peak Area Recreation Concept committee. He creates commercial children's and adult games and holds several patents.

John Benson served as an infantry platoon leader in Vietnam, receiving decorations for valor and merit. He served as president of the Cerebral Palsy organization, was a director of Children's Services of Jacksonville, Inc., (Ronald McDonald House), and participated in leadership programs in scouting, YMCA Indian Guides, and the children's ministry of his church.

"The law is always approaching, and never reaching consistency. It will become entirely consistent only when it ceases to grow," stated Justice Oliver Wendell Holmes, *Common Law* 36 (1881). Kraemer and Kendall believes Mr. Holmes' remarks are timeless in the practice of law as they help clients build bridges from the past to the future.

Van Briggle Art Pottery

Although Van Briggle Art Pottery has received the world's highest awards, it does not take a connoisseur to appreciate its unique and unsurpassed beauty any more than it takes an artist to appreciate the magnificent beauty of the Pikes Peak region.

Van Briggle Art Pottery was established in 1900, one year after Mr. Van Briggle arrived in Colorado Springs from Cincinnati, where he had studied and trained at the famous Rookwood Pottery. A short time later, his fiance, Anne Gregory Van Briggle, joined him in Colorado Springs, and together they created a tradition in fine art pottery. At age thirty-five, he died of tuberculosis, but his tradition lives on.

Known throughout the world, Van Briggle is proud to have early pieces displayed in such prestigious museums as the Metropolitan in New York, and the British and the Victoria and Albert museums in London.

Each year, tens of thousands of visitors enjoy a free tour of the production areas of the pottery, where they see artisans working on the beautiful creations at various stages of completion.

The current home of "The Pottery" is, and has been for nearly forty years, the original stone roundhouse for the Midland Terminal Railroad. Built in 1889, the imposing structure is on the National Register of Historic Places, and it is certainly one of the most well-known landmarks of the city.

Artus Van Briggle was born in Felicity, Ohio, on March 21, 1869. He was of Holland Dutch extraction, tracing his ancestry back to the celebrated artists of the Flemish School of Painting of the sixteenth and seventeenth centuries. Despite ill health, Artus went, at the age of seventeen, to Cincinnati, Ohio, studying under Carl Langenbeck of the Aaron Pottery, and later working under Mrs. Bellamy Storer of the Rookwood Pottery. He went to Paris in 1893 and studied at the Julian Art Academy under the two great masters, Jean Paul Laurens and Benjamin Constant. He also studied at the Beaux Arts where he met Anne Lawrence Gregory in 1894. They became engaged in 1895.

Anne Gregory Van Briggle was born in Plattesburg, New York, on July 11, 1868. She was taken to Paris by her mother in 1894, and was entered in the Beaux Arts, where she met Artus Van Briggle, both students in painting. A portrait which Anne painted of Artus during that time may be seen at the Van Briggle Art Pottery. Anne and Artus were married in 1903, and in 1904 his death occurred on July fourth.

KKTV-11

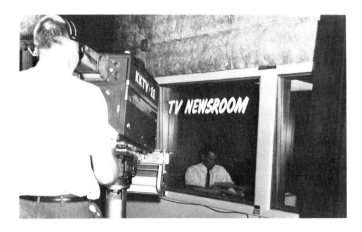

Technology has radically changed the appearance and presentation of KKTV news since these 1958 photos were taken.

Royal weddings, assassinations, floods, fires, and congressional hearings have all become commonplace in southern Colorado households via the television. But it was only thirty-five years ago, when Jim Russell founded KKTV-11, on December 7, 1952, that the first television signal was broadcast in southern Colorado from atop Cheyenne Mountain.

The first ever telecast was originally to take place at KKTV's modest studio on Mill Street. Civic dignitaries had gathered there to participate in a brief inaugural program. But typical of Colorado weather, the highly-publicized broadcast was foiled by a winter storm that interfered with microwave transmission. Undaunted, the station engineers packed up a studio camera and transported it to the top of Cheyenne Mountain in time for the heralded 6:00 pm debut—an hour broadcast of a hand-crafted test pattern on a piece of scrap wood.

As competition sprouted and grew, KKTV began aggressively broadcasting 6½ hours a day. Not long by today's standards, but much of that programming, including commercials, was broadcast live. The logistics

involved with developing film for local broadcast made live programming such as "Kay's Kitchen" and "Sheriff Jim" prevalent television fare at that time. Filmed CBS network programming arrived at KKTV only after a station to station sojourn across the country, creating broadcast delays of two and three weeks.

Despite these early technological limitations, KKTV's newsroom has traditionally been staffed with respected professionals. The dean of southern Colorado broadcasters for over three decades, Hal Kennedy, news anchor and assistant general manager, is recognized as having been anchorman and news director at one station longer than anyone else nationwide, dating to 1956. His experience brings long-term credibility to a market which has witnessed many changing faces behind its news desks.

After serving in World War II, Kennedy attended the American Institute of the Air in Minneapolis before

Hal Kennedy has been a news broadcaster with KKTV-11 since 1956.

entering radio and then television. He worked for broadcasting stations in North Dakota and Iowa before coming to Colorado Springs in 1956. Since that time KKTV News has won a long string of national, regional, and local awards for excellence in news and documentaries. "11 News at 5:30," which Kennedy co-anchored with Sandra Mann through 1989, still draws the strongest viewership in the region.

General manager Jim Lucas attributes KKTV's success to its continued commitment to southern Colorado. "We want the people of southern Colorado to know that we are more than a switch that they turn off and on in their living rooms. We are real people with a real stake in the positive growth of this region." KKTV is proud of its past and is working hard to create a strong future in this area.

Highland Properties

Cheyenne Hills

Highland Properties, Inc., is a fully integrated, closely managed company with a diverse portfolio of interests and projects. With a full-time staff sharing expertise in development, project analysis, architecture, construction, management, leasing, and finance, Highland Properties has the resources and ability to manage a project from preliminary planning stages through build-out, lease-up, and subsequent property management, with the highest degree of professionalism.

Highland Properties, Inc., and its affiliated companies, have been active in developing custom, residential, commercial, and multi-family communities for the past eighteen years in Colorado Springs, and specializes in syndication, asset management, development, manufactured housing, architecture and construction, and marketing. Starting with their in-house architectural design and development division all the way through the property management division, Highland possesses all the expertise necessary to see any project from commencement to completion.

Highland Properties' development projects are known for their insight and innovation, a result of over a decade's experience in the field. From the acquisition of raw land through the design, construction, marketing, lease-up and management phases, the company is sensitive to both the natural environment and the client's wishes. Finding solutions to potential development problems is a hallmark of the Highland Properties development team, as is a total approach to the construction management process. Project control, coordination, and administration ensure the client an attractive, functional, and technically-sound development product.

National Prebuilt Manufacturing Company, founded in 1983, is a division of Highland that designs and produces factory-built homes which combine the affordability of a manufactured home with many of the amenities of a traditional home. The company's commitment to high quality, attention to detail, and emphasis on customer satisfaction have made them highly competitive within the southwestern marketplace.

With a reputation for success and creativity that is respected throughout the industry, Highland Properties' award-winning architects and experienced project managers consistently set the trends in design and construction. Known for innovative ideas that are also cost-effective, the company combines a commitment to value engineering with an understanding of construction and production. Land planning, space planning, and building design are all coordinated with engineering disciplines, governmental regulations and replating/rezoning concerns, ensuring that all Highland Properties projects are as technically-sound as they are aesthetically pleasing.

The Park at Kissing Camels

A Highland Properties project isn't fully realized until it is fully utilized, leased, or sold; therefore, marketing is viewed as an integral step in the development process. Skilled and experienced in developing marketing plans, business plans, and feasibility studies, the Highland Properties team combines their development and brokerage expertise with an intimate knowledge of market conditions and trends. The goal is to generate transactions that are mutually beneficial and mutually profitable.

Highland Properties is a comprehensive real estate development resource, with broad experience, quality personnel, and an aggressive, hands-on approach to development.

Berry and Boyle

During the 1980s, Boston-based Berry and Boyle emerged as one of the nation's leading development-management firms specializing in joint venture partnerships of high-quality residential properties.

Investment specialists and development managers of nearly $200 million in real estate assets nationwide, Berry and Boyle recognized Colorado Springs as a city with a high quality of life, a diversified economy, a steady population growth, a consistent pattern of corporate inmigration, and prestigious, name address locations in upper-income neighborhoods suited to the development of luxury residential communities.

Berry and Boyle principals Richard G. Berry and Stephen B. Boyle entered the Colorado Springs market in the early eighties and established joint venture relationships with two of the city's most prominent developers—Highland Properties, Inc., and David R. Sellon & Company.

The result: Five outstanding residential communities featuring Broadmoor Pines, a luxury rental community developed with Highland Properties on the lower slope of Cheyenne Mountain which earned a 1989 Gold Nugget award from the Pacific Coast Builders Conference as one of the top five apartment projects in the west, and first-place honors for Best Multi-Family Community in the 1989 MAME awards sponsored by the Housing and Building Association of Colorado Springs/El Paso County.

Other Berry and Boyle properties in Colorado Springs include The Pines on Cheyenne Creek, just minutes from the world-famous Broadmoor Hotel in the southwest section of the city and winner of second-place honors in the 1989 MAME awards; and Autumn

Broadmoor Pines

Ridge, located in the city's prestigious Pinecliff section on the northwest side. Both were developed with Highland Properties.

The firm's latest endeavor is a 281-acre master planned land venture for the development of luxury single-family homesites with David R. Sellon & Company on the lower slope of Cheyenne Mountain, not far from Broadmoor Pines.

Formed in 1983, the firm's roots date back to 1975 when its principals founded EF Hutton's Real Estate Investment Department which engaged in over $500 million of residential and commercial real estate investments nationwide.

Berry and Boyle brings together quality-minded developers and value-oriented investors, organizes joint ventures, and plays a co-development role to maintain a property's quality and profitability. Because its principals and key management personnel enjoy such rich and diverse real estate backgrounds, Berry and Boyle becomes involved in every aspect of a project from the outset, its activities typically involving everything from market analysis, site selection and planning, to architectural design, interior merchandising, and full-scale marketing and property management.

Berry and Boyle, headquartered in the Boston suburb of Wellesley Hills, maintains other award-winning residential communities in Phoenix, Scottsdale, and Tucson, and has plans on the drawing board for future developments in several other markets throughout the country.

The Pines on Cheyenne Creek

Flying W Ranch

The Flying W Ranch is a working, mountain cattle ranch that has specialized in western food and entertainment since 1953. In the high season, the ranch entertains and serves dinner to over a thousand persons nightly. The Flying W has a winning combination of beautiful natural surroundings, an authentic old western town, mouth-watering food, and an outstanding western stage show. The ranch specializes in groups and conventions from sixty to fourteen hundred persons.

It all started in 1947 when Don Wilson bought the old Douglass Homestead northwest of Colorado Springs. The land was originally owned by William Palmer, the founder of Colorado Springs, and is adjacent to Palmer's Glen Eyrie.

Don made the move from his former ranching operation in Kansas. His wife, Minnie, daughters Marian and Marietta, as well as his son-in-law, Russ Wolfe, came with him. Russ and Marian lived on the ranch and helped with the ranching operations.

During the summer months, Russ rented horses. The ride caused appetites to stir and folks were mighty hungry when they returned to the ranch house. Some evenings the group would be small enough for Marian to invite the riders to share potluck. This lead to a *great idea*.

Ride and eat at night—three dollars for the entire evening. Marian found the largest pots and pans around and cooked for the riders while Russ was on the trail with them. The whole thing started with eleven paying guests attending the first night. Nowadays, the ranch serves 150,000 folks annually.

Russ and Marian have three daughters, Terry, Sunny, and Leigh Ann. The girls are very much involved with the ranch. Terry takes care of all the buying, staffing, and arranging of the twelve gift shops, each with a museum theme, in the old western town. Sunny takes care of all the group tours and reservations, a big job since the ranch has around five hundred tour companies that regularly come to the ranch. Leigh Ann is in business in New York City, but she still comes back several times a year to her real home, the ranch.

There is seating inside for fourteen hundred persons. In case mother nature is not kind, there is also a heated inside area with identical seating. The Flying W is famous for its delicious cowboy fare, chuckwagon suppers. After every meal at the ranch, the guests are entertained by the Flying W Wranglers. This is one of the very best western stage shows in the world. The Wranglers specialize in beautiful three and four part vocal harmonies about the romantic American cowboy. Their voices are outstanding, and their western humor is very entertaining.

In the wintertime, the western food and fun continues in the beautiful winter steakhouse. The steakhouse has thirty foot high Indian murals that are works of art. You can choose from several entrees, which include our famous Kansas City steak, Bar-B-Que pork ribs, beef ribs, or chicken, and flame-grilled trout. You can also get your favorite beer, wine, or cocktail from the one hundred year old picketwire bar. The steakhouse was formerly the Ute Theater in downtown Colorado Springs. It was built in 1929 and torn down in 1968. Russ and Marian loved the old theater, and bought all the old fixtures, carved woodwork, ticket booth, and furniture piece by piece at auction, and rebuilt it at the ranch.

Even with the focus on food and entertainment, the Flying W still has cattle at the home ranch and has expanded the cattle operation into the San Luis Valley. The second ranch is about four miles northwest of Del Norte, Colorado.

In 1989, the Wilson ranch and the Flying W Ranch were acknowledged by the Historical Society of the Pikes Peak Region, for preserving Colorado history.

The Penrose–St. Francis Healthcare System

The Penrose–St. Francis Healthcare System is southern Colorado's largest and most comprehensive healthcare provider. Comprised of three major Colorado Springs healthcare institutions—Penrose Hospital, Penrose Community Hospital, and St. Francis Hospital—the system's history reflects the rich past of the Pikes Peak region it serves.

St. Francis was Colorado Springs' first hospital, founded in 1887 by four Sisters of St. Francis of Perpetual Adoration from Lafayette, Indiana. Over the years, St. Francis has grown and evolved, in response to advances in medical science and community needs. Yet the tradition of interdependence and mutual support between Colorado Springs and St. Francis continues to this day.

Penrose Hospital was founded in 1889 as Glockner Sanitorium, fulfilling the dying wish of Albert Glockner to establish an institution for care of tuberculosis patients. In 1893, The Sisters of Charity of Cincinnati, Ohio, assumed the operation of the sanitorium. In 1900, faced with mounting expenses, the Sisters raised

Glockner Sanitorium and Hospital, forerunner of today's 372-bed Penrose Hospital, as it appeared in 1923.

sufficient funds from the community to pay all outstanding debts. In the years that followed, Penrose grew and expanded its capabilities, emerging as a major Colorado healthcare leader. In 1978, the Sisters of Charity purchased Colorado Springs Community Hospital, an 88-bed institution located in the vibrant, heavily populated northeast sector of the city. Renamed Penrose Community Hospital, this facility has become a dynamic, family-oriented healthcare center.

The year 1988 was a milestone year for these three

Colorado Springs hospitals. As a result of the 1987 agreement between the Sisters of Charity and Sisters of St. Francis to consolidate their healthcare systems and facilities nationwide, The Penrose–St. Francis Healthcare System was created. Effectively consolidating the facilities, personnel, and resources of Penrose, Penrose Community, and St. Francis hospitals, the System presents an exciting opportunity to meet the healthcare needs of southern Colorado well into the twenty-first century. With a combined total of 664 inpatient beds, the System's three hospitals accounted for nearly seventeen thousand inpatient and outpatient surgeries, over fifty-five thousand emergency room visits and over five thousand births in the first year after the consolidation.

The key to this consolidation is the preservation of each hospital's unique strengths and character. St. Francis is most notable for its accredited trauma center; Penrose Hospital for its cancer, cardiac, and rehabilitation programs; and Penrose Community Hospital for its family-oriented maternity care.

The history of The Penrose–St. Francis Healthcare System is a classic example of the symbiotic relationship that is shared by a community and its healthcare institutions. The Penrose St. Francis Healthcare System looks forward to continuing this mutually beneficial relationship in its second century, as the System grows and expands to meet the challenges of advancing technologies and changing community needs.

St. Francis Hospital, pictured here in 1929, was Colorado Springs' first hospital.

The Broadmoor

Outstanding service, extraordinary dedication, exquisite cuisine—these are the time honored traditions of The Broadmoor. Few hotels in the world today come close to matching the regal setting, luxurious accommodations, and diversified activity that are found at this vacationer's paradise.

It was, according to the Sunday society column of Colorado Springs' leading newspaper, the largest, most glittering, gala social event of the town's whole forty-seven year history. The new Broadmoor Hotel had formally opened with a dinner dance on Saturday, June 29, 1918. More than two hundred guests sat down to a dinner of Broadmoor Trout au Bleu, Braised Sweetbreads aux Perles du Perigord, Boneless Royal Squab, Souffle Glace, and Comtesse de Cornet.

Mr. and Mrs. C. L. Tutt gave the official and the largest party of the evening. Among their guests were Mr. and Mrs. Spencer Penrose. The hotel was a blaze of light and color as the ladies in evening gowns circulated through the flower-filled rooms, decorated with lilies, roses, and sweet peas. Two orchestras played for dancing couples in the gilt and crystal ballroom, and couples drifted out for a breath of Colorado air. The mood of the evening was one of gaiety, the affair a tremendous success. The people of Colorado Springs were proud of The Broadmoor; they had been pleased that Spencer Penrose had built such a fine pleasure spot for the city.

Every facet of Penrose's personality, every project he undertook carries its load of legends; the origins of the Broadmoor is no exception. A constant traveler and frequenter of some of the world's most famous hotels and spas, Penrose was determined "to build the finest hotel in the United States." On April 13, 1916, the *Gazette* reported that "Colorado Springs and New York capital-

ists" were going to build a new, deluxe hotel which would be designed by a famous hotel architect. It was to be four stories, of white stucco, on the west side of Broadmoor Lake. There would be fine shops, beautiful landscaping, an ice rink, and facilities for polo, tennis, golf, swimming, and boating. Gourmet food and the finest wines and liquors would be served.

On May 11, the *Gazette* named C. M. MacNeill, A. E. Carlton, and Penrose as the purchasers of the property to be developed. Frederick J. Sterner of New York, the architect who planned the Antlers in Colorado Springs and the Greenbriar in West Virginia, had been hired to design the great structure. He immediately decided the hotel should be placed on the east side of the lake, with an "Italian effect," and probably of pinkish stucco, the front to have three forty-foot arches capped by a balustrade. His tenure lasted only until September, when Penrose decided that Sterner's conception was too elaborate and dismissed him.

In November 1916, Penrose hired the architectural firm Warren and Wetmore of New York, who had designed Grand Central Station, and the Biltmore, Ritz-Carlton, Vanderbilt, and Belmont hotels in New York City. C. L. Wetmore agreed with Sterner's vision, and interestingly enough, it is that vision of the Broadmoor that can be seen today. Actual construction began

about May 20, 1917, and as the work progressed into the spring of 1918, an army of skilled artisans from the art centers of Europe and other foreign countries had decorated the walls, ceilings, and floors for the public rooms.

On June 1, 1918, the hotel opened with an informal dinner dance party, with the "big blow-out," in Penrose's words, scheduled for Saturday, June 29. Guest rooms were ready for occupancy by June 10 and a steady flow of guests began to arrive. During its early years, the Penroses pampered their hotel more than they were ever to do again. Paintings, sculptures, rugs, fine pieces of furniture flowed back to the hotel as they shopped around the world from Hong Kong to Paris.

Inseparable from the names of Broadmoor and

Penrose is that of Tutt, Charles L., Jr., and his sons, Thayer and Russell, the son and grandsons, respectively, of Penrose's original partner, Charles L., Sr., who died in 1909. Charles Jr., was in his late twenties when he became Penrose's indispensable associate in the Broadmoor project in 1916. Tutt, with his sound judgment and comprehensive grasp of detail, held the project together during Penrose's long and frequent absences from Colorado Springs. After Mr. Penrose died in 1939, Charles Tutt actively managed all operations. When Mrs. Penrose died in 1956, his sons, Russell and Thayer, gradually assumed their father's

responsibilities. Thus, the Broadmoor is the creation of four men: Spencer Penrose, who had the idea and the money, and the two generations of Tutts, who provided continuity and tradition unbroken for half a century.

Set beside its lake and rising against the dark blue-green of Cheyenne Mountain, The Broadmoor was to be refined and elaborated as the years went by, but the basic structure and the style were never to be changed. In 1961, The Broadmoor added the 144 room Broadmoor South and an all purpose hall named the Broadmoor International Center which functions as an exhibit hall, ballroom, and banquet hall. In the spring of 1976, Broadmoor West, a 150-room addition to the existing four hundred rooms, and Broadmoor South Golf Course, the resort's third 18-hole layout, were added to the complex. Constructed adjacent to the International Center to form The Broadmoor Conference Center, Colorado Hall was completed in the fall of 1982, enabling The Broadmoor to offer convention groups the most modern and extensive facility of any resort in the world.

With world-famous, award-winning restaurants, unsurpassed recreation and cultural facilities, and a shop-

ping complex on the par of Fifth Avenue, The Broadmoor has received the coveted Mobil five-star rating since 1960. Modern comfort and convenience for the contemporary traveler blend elegantly with the historic old world charm of the past, and the unique heritage of The Broadmoor is evident throughout the stately lobbies, beautifully appointed guest rooms, and lavishly decorated suites. Today's Broadmoor continues to build on its reputation as a grand resort hotel, a convenient blend of modern facilities and gracious accommodations that cannot be found anywhere else.

El Pomar Foundation

Home of El Pomar Foundation since its dedication May 10, 1958, the El Pomar Executive Office Building proudly displays a statue of its founder, Spencer Penrose, by noted western sculptor, Dr. Avard Fairbanks.

The modern structure of the Colorado Springs Community Health Center was made possible by a $2.5 million grant from El Pomar Foundation in 1988, believed to be the largest grant of its kind ever awarded a private, non-profit community health service agency.

The history of El Pomar Foundation is inexorably entwined with the life story of Spencer Penrose, its founder. Mr. Penrose arrived in Colorado Springs in 1892 to visit his boyhood friend from Philadelphia, Charles L. Tutt. "Spec," as he was called by his close friends, was the youngest of four brothers, all of whom were Harvard graduates. Each brother became successful in his chosen field, whether it be geology, politics, medicine, or mining. After his arrival in Colorado, "Spec" joined with Charles Tutt in real estate and mining in Cripple Creek. Their most successful Colorado mining venture was the Cash-On-Delivery gold mine located near Poverty Gulch.

In 1906, Mr. Penrose married and settled in Colorado Springs. A man of vision, he built many of southern Colorado's most cherished landmarks, including the Pikes Peak Highway, Cheyenne Mountain Zoo, and the Will Rogers Shrine of the Sun. His ultimate accomplishment was the construction of The Broadmoor Hotel, a world-class resort nestled into the foothills of Colorado Springs.

These physical structures are tangible reminders of the Penrose legacy; however, his greatest gift to the state of Colorado was the creation and endowment of El Pomar Foundation in 1937. His widow, Mrs. Julie McMillan Penrose, left the bulk of her estate to the foundation at her death, as well. Since its inception, El Pomar Foundation has made grants amounting to over $115 million.

El Pomar Foundation makes grants within the state of Colorado to not-for-profit organizations and institutions which represent the fields of health, arts and humanities, human services, athletics, religion, and education. Its geographical representation is statewide, ranging from the tiny town of Creede, whose repertory theater received a grant in 1988, to sprawling metropolitan Denver, which is home of the Denver Museum of Natural History, a grant recipient in 1989.

In 1989, the Trustees established the El Pomar Awards for Excellence and were gratified to have many prestigious Coloradans serve on its first Selection Commission. These awards are to recognize excellence in many fields served by the non-profits in the state of Colorado.

The foundation is administered by a five-member Board of Trustees which includes Mr. Russell T. Tutt, Mr. Ben S. Wendelken, Mr. Karl E. Eitel, Mr. William J. Hybl, and Mr. R. Thayer Tutt, Jr.

Holly Sugar Corporation

Today, Holly operates eight sugarbeet processing factories: two in Wyoming, one in Montana, one in Texas, and four in California. The broad geographical spread gives the company a competitive edge in the beet sugar industry.

It was the summer of 1905; citizens in the town of Holly were concerned and rumors were gaining momentum. In an attempt to squelch the hearsay that Holly Sugar Company might not go through with plans to complete its sugarbeet processing factory, the company raised a lone flag over the desolate prairies of southeastern Colorado. The rumors proved to be unfounded and Holly's first factory was completed in time for the sugarbeet harvest of 1905. Production that first year was 60,000 hand-sewn, 100-pound bags of sugar. A humble beginning for a company that now has operations—including sugarbeet processing factories, research facilities, and marketing offices—in a dozen different cities. Holly's annual production now averages 1.35 billion pounds of sugar.

Holly Sugar's growth was almost immediate. A year after it was established, the company built its second factory in Swink, Colorado.

Several years later, William M. Wiley, president and general manager at the time, and one of the company's founders, expanded into southern California by ordering the construction of a beet sugar factory in Huntington Beach. The factory was completed in time to handle the sugarbeet crop of 1911, the same year that Holly's main offices relocated to Denver. In 1915, Holly made its first venture into Wyoming

Holly's development caught the attention of wealthy Colorado businessman, A. E. Carlton. In 1916, Carlton and his associates acquired Holly Sugar Company and changed the name to Holly Sugar Corporation.

The company grew dramatically under Carlton's leadership as president. By either constructing new plants or acquiring them from other sugar companies, Holly Sugar added ten new factories to its list of operations between 1916 and 1931.

Besides the eight beet sugar factories in operation today, Holly Sugar has owned twelve other factories during its eighty-four year history. For a variety of reasons, operations were shut down. Holly had to close the Alvarado, California, factory in 1967 because housing developments and shopping centers took root in the once-lush sugarbeet fields. In Huntington Beach, the discovery of oil on Holly's property led to the plant closure. Depressed sugar prices, the lack of a stable national sugar policy, and farming difficulties were also contributing factors to shutdowns over the years.

Throughout its history, Holly also ventured into other business opportunities, including livestock feeding operations, oil production, and refining. The company's research facilities and sugarbeet seed processing operation continue to operate today.

In 1923, Holly's main offices were moved to Colorado Springs because A.E. Carlton was tired of the daily commute to Denver. Since 1905, Holly Sugar has grown from a single factory slicing six hundred tons of beets a day to a system with an average total daily slicing capacity of over forty thousand tons.

Early in 1988, Imperial Sugar Company acquired Holly Sugar as a wholly-owned subsidiary and Imperial Holly Corporation was established. Robert C. Hanna, president and chief executive officer, states: "Combining the capabilities of Imperial's cane sugar refinery with Holly's sugarbeet operations is advantageous in today's marketplace. We're now in a more balanced position than probably any other sugar company in America."

Imperial Holly Corporation now looks toward the future secure in the strength of its past. Well over two hundred years of experience in the sugar industry resulted when Imperial Sugar and Holly Sugar joined forces. With credentials of that magnitude, the future for Imperial Holly Corporation certainly looks sweet.

Colorado Tech

Colorado Tech was founded in 1965 as the Colorado Electronic Training Center to serve the needs of the high tech community when companies began moving to the Colorado Springs area. It was first located in the original TRW building in Colorado Springs, employing just ten people. Early on it was relocated to the skating rink in Manitou Springs, and in the mid–seventies, to 655 Elkton Drive in Colorado Springs. In 1987, Colorado Tech moved into its all-new campus at 4435 North Chestnut in Colorado Springs.

Colorado Tech's mission is to provide first-class, college level, career-oriented education by providing real world, state-of-the-art skills in selected technical fields. As such, Tech maintains its focus on teaching, keeps current and relevant its academic programs through active participation with the business community, and provides students with support services in career planning, academic advising, financial assistance, and job placement. Just as important, it provides students with an educational background broad enough to enable them to adapt to a changing environment, and to continue their education and training in response to their

changing needs and those of industry.

With 113 instructors and staff, Colorado Tech now offers degrees in computer science, computer information systems, defense systems management, logistic systems management, electrical and computer engineering, electronic engineering technology, and biomedical engineering technology. Professional Enhancement Certificate programs are offered in telecommunications, configuration and data management, control systems, technical writing, quality assurance management, and ADA and software engineering.

Colorado Tech has traditionally responded to the needs of industry. In the early years, training was provided in electronics and biomedical electronics leading to a certificate. The programs offered grew and two-year associates degrees, and later, four-year B.S. degrees were awarded. The college now offers Masters degrees in computer science and management. Colorado Tech was one of the first colleges to offer courses in solar engineering technology, and now offers one of the only degree programs nationwide in defense systems management. It is the only college with an accredited

program in CALS, (Computer Aided Acquisition and Logistics Support), a new language that the Pentagon requires from client-industry officials.

Colorado Tech is a private four-year college which is regionally accredited by the North Central Association of Colleges and Schools (NCA), and has specific programs professionally accredited by the Accreditation Board for Engineering and Technology, Inc. (ABET). Graduates from Colorado Tech clearly find successful careers in industries that are leading the way in advanced technology in the United States, with over 95 percent of graduates being placed within three months of receiving their degree.

Colorado Tech is committed to excellence and takes pride in its focused delivery of education: each student is treated like a customer; faculty and students remain on a first name basis; classrooms have only thirty-two seats in each lecture hall; a special phone is in the student hallway for students to use to make contact with any faculty member or dean. The college stresses application of technology; the textbook and the hands-on examples in the weekly labs bring the real world to the

student. All labs have twenty-four stations to insure the student will have access to a equipment ratio of 1:1 and faculty ratio of 24:1. Laboratories are available to students six days a week and no one waits in line.

In 1988, Colorado Tech announced a new million dollar "I Have A Dream" scholarship program for minority and disadvantaged youth in the Pikes Peak region. Through support of the NAACP and the minority coalition in Colorado Springs, the focus of the scholarship program is to assist qualifying high school students who have demonstrated the desire and scholastic ability to pursue an advanced technological education, with full-term tuition towards the completion of a four-year degree.

Colorado Tech is proud of its academic environment. With up-to-date equipment, comprehensive and practical academic programs, and attractive surroundings, Colorado Tech provides a challenging and exciting atmosphere for students.

Ent Federal Credit Union

The current headquarters of Ent Federal Credit Union.

The original office building in 1957.

Serving the financial needs of its members since 1957, Ent Federal Credit Union has become one of the premier financial institutions in Colorado. Originally chartered on March 7, 1957, at Ent Air Force Base in Colorado Springs, Ent has grown from its original fifty-one members to over 100,000 members.

Early in 1957, a group of individuals assigned to Ent Air Force Base, located in the 1500 block of East Boulder, petitioned the Bureau of Federal Credit Unions to issue a Credit Union Charter for the military and civilian personnel assigned to Ent Air Force Base and Peterson Field. Ent was named for Maj. Gen. Uzal Ent, a bomber pilot during World War II who participated in low-level bombing raids in Italy, Greece, and Romania. In 1944, Gen. Ent was involved in a plane crash which left him paralyzed. He worked to improve care for the handicapped and wrote a book, *What's My Score*, which offered encouragement to other paralyzed individuals. He died on March 5, 1948, at the age of forty-seven.

After the issuance of the charter to Ent Federal Credit Union, a period of rapid growth began. From that original fifty-one members and three thousand dollars in assets, the Credit Union has grown to over 100,000 members and almost $500 million in assets. From its humble beginnings in an office shared by the base commissary, with one employee, the Credit Union now has eight offices and over 270 employees. From a financial institution offering only savings accounts and loans, Ent now offers a wide variety of financial services, including Audio Response, Mortgage Loans, Visa Debit and ATM Cards, and Certificates of Deposit.

When Ent Air Force Base closed in 1976, the city of Colorado Springs leased the property to the Olympic Training Center. The main office of Ent Federal Credit Union then moved to our current main office at 805 North Murray Boulevard. Today Ent has, in addition to its main office, a facility at Peterson Air Force Base; Flintridge and Academy; in the Bon and Southgate Shopping centers; on Woodmen Road; on Jet Wing, behind the Mission Trace Shopping Center; and the Hope Coronado branch on East Costilla.

Providing outstanding financial services to its members is the goal of Ent Federal Credit Union. Ent is a true representative of the Credit Union motto, "People Helping People."

First United Methodist Church

In July of 1871, a small group of Christians gathered in the home of Gen. and Mrs. William J. Palmer to begin a Sunday School. In October, that group consisting of twenty-five members was formally organized into the first church in the new town of Colorado Springs. That little house church has grown through the years to become the four thousand member First United Methodist Church, now housed in a magnificent building occupying the western block of Nevada between Boulder and St. Vrain. And although many other congregations now use the word "first" in their title, members of this congregation may be excused for continuing to refer to First United Methodist Church as "First Church."

From the beginning, this congregation has been an active and progressive force in the development of the city, and from its membership have come leaders who have helped shape the city as a humane and beautiful habitat for living. Still in the forefront of community ministries, from Ecumenical Social Ministries to the Urban League, from Goodwill Industries to Scouting, from the Children's Center to Golden Weds, from families to singles, First Church is a Christian center where visitors are never strangers and where the difference is worth the distance.

Long known for its excellence in music and worship, First Church has more than twenty music and drama groups for all ages, and its pulpit has gained an international reputation. Dr. Gerald Trigg, senior minister since 1980, has followed such pulpit giants as Dr. Ben Lehmberg, Dr. Larry Lacour, and Bishop Calvin McConnell. Dr. Trigg has served as the featured speaker in events across the nation and in the British Isles. He recently was preacher for a month at St. Giles Cathedral in Edinburgh, Scotland, and was featured on the BBC. He appears several times weekly on local television programs.

It is not surprising that visitors to the region seek to include a "Sunday at First Church." Nor is it surprising to find those who settle in our region are making themselves at home at First United Methodist Church.

Cheyenne Mountain Nursing Center

Great moments in Colorado and American history are relived daily in the halls and rooms of Cheyenne Mountain Nursing Center.

This generation of Americans who call Cheyenne Mountain home has made significant contributions to the growth and development of this region and the nation as a whole. Among them are:

• Maj. Gen. Robert Lynn Copsey, pioneer aviator who held pilot's license No. 29—signed by Orville Wright of the famed Wright Brothers. A friend of Charles Lindbergh, Copsey pushed off the *Spirit of St. Louis* on its historic trans-Atlantic flight.

• Earl "Red" Blaik, who became a legend as a football coach at the United States Military Academy when his Army teams dominated the polls as the nation's best year after year.

• Author and painter Helen Cogswell Trostel. Her book, *All Those Dam People*, chronicled the rugged and bawdy times of dam–building on the Arkansas River.

Her paintings—particularly portraits and landscapes—freeze in time scenes and people from an important period of growth in Colorado.

The list could go on.

Cheyenne Mountain Nursing Center actually began with a national focus. When it opened its doors on November 24, 1974, noted radio and television commentator Paul Harvey was principal speaker. He pointed out that the facility was an outstanding example of private enterprise meeting public need.

The center was developed by Robert W. Rieger and Associates, and opened with 120 beds. In 1985, the center was remodeled and expanded. Today, it offers 180 beds of long-term care in a beautiful and loving environment.

Life Care Centers of America, a nationwide management company with ninety-five nursing centers in twenty-six states, took over operation of Cheyenne Mountain in 1981.

"It is the commitment of Cheyenne Mountain to be the premier provider of long-term health care in Colorado Springs and El Paso County," said Mary Estlow, executive director. "It is our desire to be the facility of choice. Our programs, services, and facilities must be designed and operated with superior quality in order to satisfy the needs of our patients."

Cheyenne Mountain's "values statement" places its emphasis on patient care.

care needs of this community, and we are always ready to direct our resources to meet those needs. We practice good corporate citizenship in this community, maintaining communications with the various publics we serve and participating actively in community affairs, particularly related to health care."

The long-term care industry is growing rapidly to accommodate the needs of the populace, Estlow said.

"Nationally, health care professionals estimate that the demand for nursing home beds will increase by 50 percent between now and the year 2000—only eleven years away. Cheyenne Mountain Nursing Center will always be on the cutting edge of responding to the needs of this area, and doing so in a professional and loving way.

"After all, every person who enters these doors and is entrusted to our care is a precious part of history. They deserve the best for their unique contributions to the welfare of all of us."

"We believe patients are our highest priority," Estlow said. "We are dedicated to the preservation of dignity, self-respect, and patient rights in a loving and caring environment. We practice the patient-centered approach to care in which the total health needs of the patient are met. The patient's family is encouraged to become closely involved with the facility in meeting the patient's needs."

Cheyenne Mountain also has a strong commitment to the community, she added.

"Our center is responsive to the long-term health

The Gazette Telegraph

The *Gazette Telegraph* had its beginning 117 years ago, when the city's founder, Gen. William J. Palmer, published the first edition of the *Out West* newspaper on March 23, 1872.

Located in the city's first two-story building, at the corner of Tejon Street and Colorado Avenue (then Huerfano Street), the newspaper was soon renamed the *Colorado Springs Gazette and El Paso County News,* and published every Saturday morning.

A major milestone was accomplished on May 1, 1878, when the first issue of the *Daily Gazette* became the city's first daily newspaper.

In 1896, Palmer sold the paper for $50,000 to a group of young men, including Cornelius Vanderbilt, Henry Russell Wray, and William McKay Barbour. The *Gazette,* which had been published daily except Mondays, became a seven-day publication.

During the first few years of the 1900s, the newspaper changed hands several times. In 1923, the *Gazette* merged with the *Evening Telegraph.* The Gazette Telegraph Company owned the paper until 1946, when it was purchased by R. C. Hoiles, founder of Freedom Newspaper, Inc.

The *Gazette Telegraph* is the second largest paper owned by Freedom Newspapers Inc., a nationwide communications company, publishing twenty-nine daily newspapers and three weekly newspapers, and operating five television stations. The corporation is headquartered in Orange County, California, and privately owned by the family successors of the late R. C. Hoiles.

The front page of the first edition of Out West *from 1872 shows dramatically how newspapers have changed.*

International Bible Society

International Bible Society Scriptures being distributed in Pakistan.

International Bible Society's lobby filled with friends, new and old, for its dedication on May 19, 1989.

On the cold evening of December 4, 1809, a small group of evangelism-minded Christians met in the home of Theodorus Van Wyck at 34 Greenwich Street in New York City. In that meeting, the International Bible Society—then known as the New York Bible Society—was born. Their goal was simple: "to extend the knowledge of the Holy Scriptures in which God has revealed the way of salvation to our lost and ruined race." Of the first Bible societies founded in America, the International Bible Society is the only one to have grown into an international ministry.

Since that time, its purpose has remained the same: "to serve the Church in evangelism by translating, publishing, and distributing God's Word so that all people everywhere may come to a saving faith in Jesus Christ." The ultimate result of every International Bible Society project—whether it be translating the Scriptures in Latin America, distributing Bibles in Africa, or assisting native evangelists in Asia—is to share the good news of Jesus Christ with lost men, women, and children.

The Bible Society is a non-profit organization that began by handing out Bibles and giving personal encouragement to dock workers in hotels, hospitals, jails, and shelters for the homeless. The founders believed that in these writings God had "revealed the way of salvation." A strong commitment to evangelism using God's Word still characterizes the International Bible Society's ministry, which moved to Colorado Springs from East Brunswick, New Jersey, in 1988.

Each year the organization distributes over 20 million Scriptures around the world. Current projects include supplying a million Bibles for African school children, 1.5 million Scriptures for believers in Eastern Europe, and over 10 million Scriptures for use in India. In the United States, the Bible Society annually provides 150,000 Bibles and New Testaments for students on high school and college campuses, homeless people and prisoners.

Recipients of the organization's Scriptures include Billy Graham, Luis Palau, Operation Mobilization, and many other Christian groups, including some headquartered in Colorado Springs. The ministry also publishes approximately half of Wycliffe Bible Translators' new Scripture translations worldwide.

The majority of the Bible Society's Scriptures are distributed free of charge, thanks to the gifts of Christians in the United States. About five million Scriptures a year are sold at or below cost to churches and individuals in the United States for their own use in evangelism. The Bible Society also sponsors evangelism/church growth seminars in local churches throughout America.

One out of every three Bibles sold today is a *New International Version*, with sales of these Bibles surpassing those of the venerated King James translation. This popular and respected translation of the Bible was commissioned by the International Bible Society in 1967 and published in 1978. It is now being distributed worldwide from Colorado Springs, and is the best-selling English translation in the world today.

When that small band of believers began over 180 years ago, their vision was not limited to simply reaching a single city with the gospel—they soon saw the need to reach beyond their immediate boundaries. Today, the International Bible Society is taking God's Word to every corner of the world, transcending the barriers of politics, geography, language, and culture.

Denver Equipment Company

The Denver Equipment Company (DENVER) started in 1927 in Denver, Colorado, by Arthur C. Daman, subsequently moved to Colorado Springs, and has been occupying four city blocks and the present foundry and manufacturing facility on South Sierra Madre since 1941.

Following periods of transition, DENVER reverted back to private ownership in February 1988, and is now the Denver Equipment Company again. The chairman of the board, Ronald A. Robinson, makes his home here in Colorado Springs and sees an encouraging, viable, and expanding company—part of a growing Colorado Springs.

With over sixty years of engineering, design, and manufacturing experience, and by offering a wide range of product lines serving a variety of industries, Denver Equipment remains one of the most respected companies in the national and international processing equipment industry. DENVER's products are found in the mineral, coal, power, chemical, pulp and paper, food, hazardous waste, and waste treatment industries, amongst others.

Being a customer–oriented, problem–solving organization, DENVER in Colorado Springs tests, designs, engineers, and builds to meet customer needs. The equipment designed and manufactured in Colorado Springs ranges from the smallest part for a pump to large processing systems. But it is the people who make the company what it is today.

The average time of employment for DENVER employees is over eleven and a half years, reflecting the pride that has characterized the company's employees since its inception in 1927, and the wealth of expertise accumulated in all departments.

The Colorado Springs company is the worldwide headquarters for DENVER with manufacturing subsidiaries in Boulder, Colorado; London, England; and Sydney, Australia, along with over forty licensees and representatives in over fifty countries around the world. Approximately 50 percent of DENVER's worldwide sales are either manufactured in, or exported into, countries other than the United States.

DENVER's business can be divided into four major segments: *Thermal Equipment:* The industrial uses for DENVER's thermal processing equipment are in the heating and cooling of ash, and coal drying for

the power industry; crystallization in the plastics industry; and drying sludge in the waste treatment industries. The HOLO-FLITE® with a variety of surface finishes is also used in the food industry for all kinds of uses from melting chocolate to drying cornflakes.

Processing Equipment: This segment targets the processing industry with everything from small laboratory sized flotation and measuring equipment to large thickeners and agitators for up to 200–foot and 63–foot diameter tanks, respectively, limeslaking systems, filters, flotation, and samplers, to mention few.

Pumping Equipment: Slurry pumping, meeting a wide variety of pumping applications from industrial wastes to coal, is DENVER's forte. DENVER's pumps are innovative and recognized as state–of–the–art. They come in sizes from a 2–inch inlet to 20–inch inlet. To equate this to common usage, a regular household faucet releases approximately two gallons of water per minute, whereas the largest of the DENVER pumps will pump the equivalent of twelve thousand faucets a minute, or in excess of twenty-four thousand gallons of slurry a minute.

Process Control and Measurement: DENVER's fourth market segment addresses the high–tech world of X-ray and laser technology through its Autometrics subsidiary. Its measurement systems and monitors for particle sizing and refractory measurement are used in the mining and steel industries.

DENVER's variety of products and industry applications are evidence of its vitality and continuing contributions to the Colorado Springs community.

AMI Industries, Inc.

AMI Industries, formerly Aircraft Mechanics, Inc., is a direct descendant of Alexander Aircraft Company, whose parent was the Alexander Film Company, a major producer of movie screen advertising from the 1920s through the 1950s. AMI is a management owned metal products manufacturer whose primary business through its fifty-seven year life has been the manufacture of aerospace products. AMI's predecessor, Alexander Aircraft, in fact manufactured complete aircraft in the late 1920s to early 1930s.

In the mid 1920s, Alexander Film decided to go into the airplane business—initially to provide aircraft for its national sales force to use. By mid-1928, Alexander Aircraft's factory was one of the largest of its kind and was capable of producing one aircraft per hour. Alexander sold approximately nine hundred Eaglerocks during the relatively few years it was produced, making it one of the principal general aviation aircraft of its time. Charles Lindberg had wanted to order one for his New York to Paris flight, but was turned down because the company was so bogged down with orders.

Alexander created a second plane called The Bullet, which was the first plane with retractable landing gear built in the United States, and was a prototype for today's sophisticated business aircraft.

While 1928 was a boom year, it was followed by the stock market crash in 1929. Alexander hung on until 1931, when it was finally forced to shut down production. In 1932, the chief engineer of Alexander, Proctor Nichols, formed a corporation called Aircraft Mechanics, Inc. This company survived the 1930s and in 1939 was awarded the first of many contracts which extended through World War II to produce engine mounts. Fol-

lowing the war, it began production of aircraft crew seating, landing gear, ground support equipment, jacks, and railroad passenger seating.

AMI was one of the pioneers in the development of aircraft ejection seats. In 1945, AMI was awarded a USAF research and development contract to undertake a study of the problems of this relatively new phase of escape and survival system.

In 1952, AMI designed, tested, and manfactured ejection seats for the B57A bomber. Subsequently, it won numerous contracts for various aircraft, and over some twenty years, AMI delivered six thousand ejection seats. In more recent years, it has designed and built all seats for the NASA space shuttles, and a wide variety of commerical and military aircraft, including the DC8, DC9, DC10, Boeing 737, 747, and Lockheed C-130.

AMI Industries is presently involved in advanced engineering design and development of aircraft crew, attendant, and helicopter seats and inertia reels, which will meet the latest FAA requirements for crash worthiness and safety. These designs also incorporate the use of fire retardant materials which minimize smoke and toxicity in the event of aircraft fires. Recent new customers for advanced design seats include British Aerospace, deHavilland (Boeing Canada), Iberian Air (Spain) and U. S. Air.

AMI Industries was purchased in March 1987 by three members of its present management team. Employment has increased 30 percent since then to over two hundred employees. Being a long-time Colorado Springs employer, it is not unusual to give out service awards for well over twenty-five years of employment. The company still occupies the same building in which its predecessor built planes.

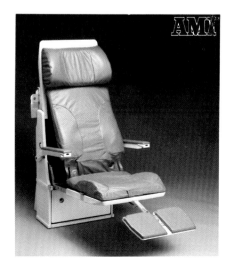

Gates Land Company

It was early 1967 when Charles C. Gates, Jr., a Colorado native, and chairman of The Gates Rubber Company, flew his helicopter over the foothills of Cheyenne Mountain. He quickly decided to buy the rolling ranch land below him with the dream of building a major expansion of the good living for which Colorado Springs is renowned. The property was a rare and beautiful area just three miles from downtown Colorado Springs, truly a once-in-a-lifetime opportunity.

Gates Land Company was established in 1968 to develop this three thousand acres into a new community called Cheyenne Mountain Ranch. Gates carefully developed a comprehensive master plan that represented the best judgment of an outstanding team of real estate professionals. Work began immediately and by the end of 1971, the first homeowner was enjoying life in the award-winning Spring Grove neighborhood. "Mrs. Miller and the Gates staff celebrated by exchanging gifts," remembers David Sunderland, President of Gates Land Company.

From the beginning, the corporate goal of Gates Land Company has been to create the finest living environment in Colorado Springs. Achieving that goal has required a major investment of resources into Cheyenne Mountain Ranch and the overall community. "For Gates to succeed, we know that Colorado Springs has to succeed," states Sunderland. "That's one reason why the Gates people spend so much time on community affairs."

Recreation is a central part of the Gates environment. Construction of The Country Club of Colorado started as the first residents settled on Cheyenne Mountain Ranch. Conceived as a family recreation center for all ages, the club opened in 1973 with the greatest array of recreation facilities ever seen in Colorado Springs, from golf and tennis to fishing and sailing. Today, this complex of year-around sports facilities offers unmatched recreation opportunities.

Contemporary families and households have remarkable diversity in their housing aspirations. Gates Land Company has responded by creating neighborhoods for almost every lifestyle. In 1972, Cheyenne Hills offered the first family living at moderate prices adjoining Quail Lake Park. Garden apartments became available the very next year at Wildridge, followed quickly by townhomes like Seventh Tee and the spectacular custom home neighborhoods of Broadmoor Hills.

During the 1980s, new and diverse living environments opened with remarkable regularity—each offering a special choice of lifestyle. Today more than thirty-five neighborhoods offer high quality living in Cheyenne Mountain Ranch. Along the way Gates Land Company has planned and built over thirty miles of roadways,

Mayor Eugene McCleary and Charles Gates, Jr., at the groundbreaking for Cheyenne Mountain Ranch in December, 1969.

constructed fifty acres of lakes, and established more than 350 acres of parks and open space. Strong protective covenants have encouraged the kind of neighborhood pride that creates lasting live-ability. The sustained effort by Gates Land Company to offer uncompromising value has attracted more than eleven thousand residents to the Ranch.

With expanding population came growing opportunities for employment. "Business executives are attracted to Cheyenne Mountain Ranch for the same good reasons people want to live here," according to Sunderland. Honeywell selected the Ranch in 1975 for its Solid State Electronics Center and brought hundreds of jobs within walking distance. Now owned by Atmel, this 240,000 square foot operation is still the largest employer on the Ranch. It has been joined by Cray Computer, the national headquarters of Junior Achievement, Cheyenne Mountain Conference Resort, and many smaller companies located across the Ranch in more than two million square feet of employment activity.

Cheyenne Mountain Ranch has become an exceptional testimonial to great western living. It is a special place, because of the natural splendor and the careful planning and thoughtful guidance by Gates Land Company for more than twenty years. According to Executive Vice President Don Davidson, "The greatest satisfaction for Gates is to know that people really enjoy living here."

Gates Land Company has charted the future for Cheyenne Mountain Ranch and invites others to discover and share this uncommon environment.

Holland & Hart

Holland & Hart, based in Denver, was formed in 1947, with two partners and two associates. Since that time the firm has grown steadily to its present size of approximately 230 full-time lawyers, the largest firm in the Rocky Mountain region. Presently offices are located in Denver, Denver Tech Center, Aspen, and Colorado Springs in Colorado; Cheyenne, Wyoming; Billings, Montana; Boise, Idaho; and Washington, D.C.

The Colorado Springs office of Holland & Hart traces its origins back to the turn of the century through two principal men—John Haney and William Spurgeon. This heritage makes it the oldest law practice in Colorado Springs.

John T. Haney (1883-1971) brought his family to Colorado Springs in 1920 from Mississippi, where he became associated with George W. Bierbauer and William S. Jackson. Mr. Biebauer died soon after, but the firm of Haney & Jackson continued until the early 1940s, when Mr. Jackson was named to the Colorado Supreme Court. John Haney's two sons, William Q. Haney (1909-1977) and J. Donald Haney, became associated with the firm which, following Judge Jackson's move to Denver, became Haney & Haney.

Joining the Haney & Haney practice in the 1940s was Irving Howbert, grandson of one of the founding fathers of Colorado Springs and the right-hand man of General William J. Palmer, the city's founder and planner. The firm was known as Haney & Howbert through the 1940s and into the 1950s, when Byron L. Akers joined the firm, to create Haney, Howbert & Akers. The firm grew and later acquired the practice of Foard, Foutch & Hunt in 1968. In 1976, ten lawyers were in the firm of Haney, Howbert & Akers, making it the largest firm in the city

at the time.

William H. Spurgeon (1867-1943) moved to Colorado Springs in the early 1900s after practicing law briefly in Creede and for some time in Cripple Creek. He served for a short time as Colorado Springs' first mayor and was a founder of the area chamber of commerce. Along with Henry C. Cassidy, Funston Clark, and his son Robert L. Spurgeon (1904-1986), the law firm of Spurgeon, Clark & Spurgeon was formed. In the 1960s, William R. Aman and Richard W. Hanes, practicing as Aman and Hanes, joined the firm, which then became Spurgeon, Aman & Hanes.

In 1976, the two law firms of Spurgeon, Aman & Hanes, and Haney, Howbert, & Akers merged to become Spurgeon, Haney & Howbert, Professional Corporation, the largest law firm in the history of Colorado Springs. From that merger has grown the present configuration, which combined its practice with that of Holland & Hart on July 1, 1986.

Historically, Holland & Hart has worked to ensure that the best available legal talent is applied to assist clients in achieving business, professional, and personal goals. Holland & Hart is engaged in a general civil practice, with half the firm's practice representing litigation activity, with substantial involvement in the traditional

areas of corporate, securities, pension, labor, antitrust, commercial, financing, business contracts, international commercial transactions, estate planning, probate, real estate, tax, administrative, legislative, patent, copyrights, trademarks, public utilities, family, personal injury, and product liability law.

Holland & Hart also has an extensive practice relating to the natural resources of the western United States, including mining, water, oil and gas, environmental law, livestock, and other agricultural and related matters. For the future, Holland & Hart continues to search for ways to effectively serve the needs of their current and future clients.

KOAA-TV 5/30

John O. Gilbert, President and General Manager

It was June 29, 1953. The TV station signed on as KCSJ-TV. It was located on Pueblo's "Big Hill," and was operated together with KCSJ Radio under the same ownership as the Pueblo *Chieftan and Star Journal.*

Although the station was an NBC affiliate licensed to serve Pueblo and the southern Colorado region, many of the programs were live, local productions. A Saturday night barn dance in the studio was one of the station's more popular shows.

The year 1959 saw the station go to full power, with the transmitter being moved from the Big Hill to a new tower high atop Baculite Mesa, making it the tallest man-made structure in the state. It was at this point that the station began broadcasting into the Colorado Springs market and was officially designated its NBC affiliate.

In 1961, KCSJ-TV was bought by KOA-TV in Denver, and the call letters were changed to KOAA-TV. Owned in part by Bob Hope, the station flourished, adding videotape technology in 1962, a microwave system from Denver in 1966, and KOAA-TV became the area's first station with local color broadcasts in 1967.

During the early seventies, the station was operated by several non-broadcast owners, resulting in a loss of some of its prestige, as well as some of its viewers.

But in 1977, KOAA-TV came under the ownership of the Evening Post Publishing Company in Charleston, South Carolina. John O. Gilbert, a former executive with the ABC Network, was brought in as general manager. Under his guidance, the station began a "full court press" into the Colorado Springs market. Gilbert saw that the reality of a dual city market demanded the station be fiercely competitive in sales, news, community service, and local programming in both cities.

The opening of a full-time Colorado Springs news and sales office, the addition of advanced news gather-

ing equipment, the initiation of a nightly editorial program, and the establishment of an active community affairs department positioned the station as an equal competitor.

In 1981, Channel 30 was added. From an antenna atop Cheyenne Mountain, Channel 30 brought a clear, clean signal to large parts of Colorado Springs that were receiving a less than adequate signal on Channel 5.

Since then, the station has installed a new Channel 5 transmitter, an advanced antenna system, new master control and production control switches, digital effects, and in 1986 became the area's first television station to broadcast in stereo.

With the completion in 1988 of the beautiful, new 5/30 Communication Building, overlooking Eighth Street and the city of Colorado Springs, KOAA-TV established an even stronger visual image within the community. The two-story, red brick structure is now the home of the "Eyewitness News" team, Studio 5/30 production, promotion, sales, and editorial departments.

The station's commitment to the community remains evident through the numerous public affairs specials it produces each year. From the "Fabulous Fourth Symphony In The Park," the action-packed "Pikes Peak Hillclimb," and the festive "Pops On Ice" presentation, to quality NBC and syndicated programming, KOAA-TV, Channels 5 & 30, continues to "Bring Home The Best" to the people in Colorado Springs.

KOAA-TV Channels 5 & 30, for two years in a row, was named the Colorado Broadcaster's choice for "Station of the Year."

Digital: Global Company

Digital Equipment Corporation is a worldwide computer solutions company committed to the Pikes Peak region since 1976.

The company first opened in Maynard, Massachusetts, in 1957, with three employees, including its current president Ken Olsen. By 1988, Digital had grown to a multi-billion dollar corporation with more than 120,000 employees in over 1,100 facilities thoughout the world. Digital provides computing solutions encompassing systems, applications, networks, hardware, software, and support services.

The company's association with the Pikes Peak region began in 1976 when a small disk manufacturing operation opened in Fountain. By April 1978, these operations were moved to a specially–built, multi-million dollar manufacturing facility in the Rockrimmon area of Colorado Springs. By the late 1980s, Digital's involvement in the Pikes Peak region had grown to more than thirty-five hundred employees at numerous facilities throughout the city.

Digital's current efforts in Colorado Springs range from operating a sophisticated, open round-the-clock Customer Support Center, to the engineering and manufacturing of mass-storage subsystems, to advanced research and development projects, to many corporate support groups and services.

Digital is a firm supporter of the local community, and is continually and intrinsically involved with the higher education institutions, civic organizations, and local efforts that keep Colorado Springs a better place to live.

The Colorado Springs Marriott

From its hilltop location in the Colorado Springs Technological Center, the Colorado Springs Marriott provides a spectacular view of the city's most famous landmark, Pikes Peak.

The nine-story, red brick hotel was opened to much fanfare in April 1989 as more than fifteen hundred people attended a lavish grand opening celebration featuring the finest in cuisine and an opulent atmosphere. With 302 deluxe guest rooms and eight suites, the Marriott boasts a striking interior design that combines the red sandstone colors so prominent in the region with other features of the American Southwest.

The Marriott traditionally offers only the finest in food and entertainment. With fresh seafood flown in from both coasts regularly, Gratzi is the hotel's seafood and pasta restaurant, providing a casual setting for breakfast, lunch, and dinner. Close by is Chats, a quiet lobby lounge with live piano music. Cahoots is a high-energy nightclub featuring live entertainment and state-of-the-art sound and lighting. Each weekday afternoon, Cahoots hosts Marriott's popular "Hungry Hour" with plenty of hot and cold hors d'oeuvres.

Offering more than 9100 square feet of meeting space, the main ballroom can accommodate receptions for 1100 or be divided into sections for smaller groups. Along with the other nearby meeting rooms, the Marriott can handle a wide range of groups for meetings, conferences, dinners, and parties.

The city's only Concierge Level is offered at the Marriott, featuring restricted elevator access for privacy, a comfortable Concierge Lounge, evening turn-down service, and a helpful concierge attendant. Guests on this floor are treated to a complimentary continental breakfast of fresh juice, fruit, cereal, yogurt, and warm pastries each morning, as well as an honor bar and complimentary hors d'oeuvres in the afternoon.

Other facilities at the Marriott include indoor and outdoor pools, a health club complete with exercise room and whirlpool, and a gift shop. Among the in-room services are cable television with HBO, CNN, ESPN, the Disney Channel, and pay-per-visit movies, room service, valet service, and a complimentary copy of USA Today delivered each morning.

The Marriott Corporation was founded in 1927 when J. Willard and Alice S. Marriott opened a nine-seat root beer stand called The Hot Shoppe in Washington D.C. Since then the company has grown into an international leader in lodging and food service. Today, Marriott is a diversified lodging and food service company with operations in all fifty states and twenty-four countries. Its businesses include over 360 hotels in all segments of the lodging market, from full-service hotels and resorts to economy motels; over two thousand institutional food and services management accounts; in-flight catering operations serving more than 140 airlines; airport terminal restaurant operations at

forty-nine domestic and four international airports; and over one thousand fast food, family, and turnpike restaurants. The Colorado Springs Marriott is owned and operated by Interstate Hotels Corporation, which is headquartered in Pittsburgh, Pennsylvania.

Seven Falls

Beautiful by day, spectacular by night, it's no wonder that the world-famous Seven Falls and the adjacent South Cheyenne Canon is known as the "Grandest Mile of Scenery in Colorado." With all the natural splendor of the Rockies—unique rock formations, a Colorado trout-filled pond at the foot of the Falls, charming chipmunks, and authentic Indian dances—Seven Falls appeals to all the senses, particularly when it becomes a nighttime fantasyland.

Over a century ago, James Hull purchased Seven Falls with the idea of creating a scenic attaction. Hull built a road through the then inaccessible canon to the Falls, and he and his sons improved the property by building a stairway to the top of the Falls. He installed a toll gate at the mouth of the canon and opened it as a scenic "ranch." The only way to get to the Falls was by carriages, horses, and burros. For twenty-five cents each, tourists, bustles, whiskers, and dusters were transported in thirteen carriages, one tallyho, and six Juberton and White buckboards.

In 1905, the Hull family sold out to C. D. Weimer

A. G. Hill

for $250,000, and as the years rolled by, more and more tourists were attracted to the Colorado Springs area. Under Weimer's ownership, more land was purchased until the property consisted of 1400 acres. Burros were used above the Falls to take tourists to Helen Hunt's grave. She had requested to be buried near "Inspiration Point," where she spent many hours writing her poetry and the book *Ramona*, later a best-seller as a popular song and even more famous as a movie. She wanted her friends to bring two stones from the canon—to place one on her grave and take one home in remembrance. That is how the huge pile of stones that mark her grave came into being. The spirit of Helen Hunt Jackson remains. The pilgrimage up the stairway beside the Falls is made by thousands annually.

Among the contributions made in recent years to the attractiveness of Colorado Springs and the Pikes Peak region are those made by Albert Galatyn Hill. A Tennessee native, Mr. Hill had lived in Colorado as a youth and attended Colorado College, where one of his classmates was Melvin Weimer. On occasions, Mr. Hill, with a group of college friends, visited the canon on moonlit nights and realized the unqiue beauty of the canon at night. It can be said that no one can improve nature. Mr. Hill, then a Dallas resident, did when he purchased the Falls in 1946.

Nature shuts off the light with the setting of the sun. Mr. Hill turned it on with the dusk. He did not improve the natural scenery, of course, but by lighting many of the outstanding formations in South Cheyenne Canon, he made it possible for spectators to enjoy the nighttime view. Then, with Hill's construction of the "Eagle Nest," an observation platform on the south wall of the canon, for the first time, all of the Seven Falls could be seen at once.

In 1948, a Christmas tradition was started of opening

Mr. R. S. Brown of Murfreesboro, Tennessee, and daughter, Mrs. C. S. Page of Pueblo, Colorado. Shown here, are the grandfather and aunt of A. G. Hill. Taken August, 1916

the canon at night free to the people of Colorado Springs. During this period, the life-sized Santa Claus, sleigh, and reindeer appears atop the Seven Falls Curio Shop. The pine trees of the inspiring canon are filled with Christmas lights. Adding to the festive holiday season are Christmas carols, played throughout the canon over the intricate sound system. As Seven Falls' annual Christmas gift to the region, this display has converted a multitude of Colorado Springs natives into winter sightseers.

Mr. Hill had a vision, and the creativity and initiative to carry out that vision. The result is that one of the most beautiful waterfalls in the world and some of the most awe-inspiring scenery—here or anywhere else—are now to be seen in the scenic grandeur at night, creating another memorable experience for visitors to take home with them.

Mr. Hill's vision, however, did not stop with Seven Falls. He acquired a 1400 acre dry and parched mesa and enhanced the City by using water not suitable for human consumption to build a luxuriant tree-lined golf course, which today is surrounded by beautiful homes with the famous view of Pikes Peak through the gateway of the Garden of the Gods. This spectacular view is associated by many with the emblem of the State of Colorado. Because of Mr. Hill's perception, many residents enjoy this choice location.

Mr. Hill was inspired by the moonlight reflection on the Garden of the Gods formation and his knowledge of the spectacular effects achievable by the lighting on the granite walls in South Cheyenne Canon. Utilizing his lighting expertise, the Kissing Camels formation was illuminated by a single powerful beam projected from the mesa property. Now the famous and unusual Kissing Camels formation is spotlighted every night.

In olden days the stage coach crossed the fringe of this mesa. There still exists a small stone bridge and an old abandoned road within thirty-seven acres which Mr. Hill donated to the Palmer Foundation. A large bronze plaque marks and describes the historical area.

Because of this area's delight in night-lighting, the city of Colorado Springs has placed a permanent light, akin to a star, atop magnificent Pikes Peak.

Colorado Springs and the Pikes Peak massif from the air, late May 1980. Photo from authors' collection

Bibliography

Abbott, Morris W., *The Pikes Peak COG Railroad,* Golden West Books, San Marino, Calif., 1972.

Carter, Carrol Joe, *Pike in Colorado,* Old Army Press, Fort Collins, Colo., 1978.

Carter, Harvey L., *Zebulon Montgomery Pike, Pathfinder and Patriot,* Dentan Printing Co., Colorado Springs, 1956.

Howbert, Irving, *Indians of the Pikes Peak Region,* Rio Grande Press, Glorieta, New Mexico, 1970.

Howbert, Irving, *Memories of a Lifetime in the Pikes Peak Region,* Rio Grande Press, Glorieta, New Mexico, 1970.

Hubbard, Richard L., and Wyatt, Danny J., *Geology of the Pikes Peak Region, Colorado,* Century One Press, Colorado Springs, 1976.

Hughes, David R., *Historic Old Colorado City,* David R. Hughes, Colorado Springs, 1978.

Hunt, Inez, and Draper, Wanetta, *Colorado Crazy Quilt,* HAH Publications, Colorado Springs, 1971.

Johnson, Emily, *The White House Ranch,* O'Brien Printing and Lithographic Press, Colorado Springs, 1972.

Larson, H. Kay Brander, *Valley of the Fountain,* Shopper Press, Fountain, Colo., 1969.

Ormes, Manley Dayton, *The Book of Colorado Springs,* Dentan Printing Co., Colorado Springs, 1933.

Pearl, Richard M., *America's Mountain,* Mineral Book Co., Colorado Springs, 1954.

Pearl, Richard M., *Landforms of Colorado,* Earth Science Publishing Co., Colorado Springs, 1975.

Pettit, Jan, *A Quick History of Ute Pass,* Little London Press, Colorado Springs, 1979.

Sommers, Herbet M., *The Story of the Big Burn of 1853-54,* Dentan & Berkeland Printing Co., Colorado Springs, 1965.

Sprague, Marshall, *Newport in the Rockies,* Sage Books, Denver, 1961.

Tutt, William Thayer, *The Broadmoor Story,* The Newcomen Society, New York, 1969.

Wilcox, Rhoda D., *The Man On The Iron Horse,* Rhoda D. Wilcox, Colorado Springs, 1959.

Index

Acknowledgements

The preparation, research of materials and writing of the text would not have been possible without the help of the following people and organizations:

The United States Army, the United States Air Force, NORAD, Bob Paul, Pat Olkiewicz and Fred Cappy of the Olympic Training Center, Adna Wilde of the Pioneers' Museum, Mary Davis of Penrose Public Library, the *Gazette Telegraph* the Pikes Peak Posse of the Westerners, the Historical Society of the Pikes Peak Region, the El Paso County Pioneer's Association, the Horticultural Arts Society, Cheyenne Cañon Research, the National Weather Service, the city of Colorado Springs, John May, Mrs. William Steer and the May Museum of Natural History, Connie Heidenreich and the Colorado Springs Chorale, Jim Mitchell and the Colorado Springs Symphony Orchestra, Christine Haigler Krall and the Broadmoor World Arena, Grant Carey and the Cave of the Winds, and photographers Jim Bates, Ollie Wicks, Ernie Ferguson, and Carol Hetzler.

Special thanks goes to Stewarts Commercial Photographers and Cloyd Brunson, and to Lee's Camera, who processed all photographs, and to Carol Hetzler who proofread the manuscript and patiently allowed this book to be written.

The Nikon camera and lens system was used for all photographic work and the Kodak system was used for film and processing.

Rosemary I. Hetzler is a native of Colorado Springs, who received her formal education in journalism and has written many published articles about local history. She worked for the Colorado Springs Chamber of Commerce and was the Historian for the Pioneers' Museum before retirement in 1984. She extensively studied Southwest Native American cultures and is an authority on the Hopi. She is an active member of the Pikes Peak Posse of the Westerners, the El Paso County Pioneer's Association, the Historical Society of the Pikes Peak Region, the Ghost Town Club, and the Colorado State Historical Society.

John Inness Hetzler, B. A. Adams State College, is a public school teacher, pianist, published composer and author. He studies natural history, particularly botany and entomology, and Colorado history extensively. He has climbed every 14,000-foot mountain in Colorado, made first ascents of several difficult rocks and explored many Colorado caves. He has been a member of the Pikes Peak Posse of the Westerners, the Historical Society of the Pikes Peak Region, the Colorado Mountain Club, the National Speleological Society, and several national entomological and botanical societies. He is married to Carol Hetzler, B.S. Colorado State University, naturalist and photographer. Their daughter Emily, represents their sixth family generation in Colorado.